A VICTORIAN LADY'S GUIDE TO LIFE

A VICTORIAN LADY'S GUIDE TO LIFE

ELSPETH MARR

EDITED BY CHRISTOPHER RUSH

Michael O'Mara Books Limited

This paperback edition first published in 2018
First published as *Aunt Epp's Guide for Life* in Great Britain in 2009 by
Michael O'Mara Books Limited
9 Lion Yard
Tremadoc Road
London SW4 7NQ

A CIP catalogue record for this book is available from the British Library.

Papers used by Michael O'Mara Books Limited are natural, recyclable products
made from wood grown in sustainable forests. The manufacturing processes
conform to the environmental regulations of the country of origin.

ISBN: 978-1-78243-892-2 in paperback format
ISBN: 978-1-78243-942-4 in ebook format

1 2 3 4 5 6 7 8 9 10

www.mombooks.com

This book contains lifestyle a
old-fashioned home remedie
relied upon as an alternative
or a registered specialist. Nei
responsibility for such advice

Designed and typeset by Ana
Cover images: shutterstock.co

Printed and bound by CPI Group (UK) Ltd, Croydon, CR0 4YY

Introduction

Elspeth Marr (1871-1947) was my great-great-aunt on my mother's side, and although she died before I was three, she remains my earliest and most vivid childhood memory. She was also our landlady, and each morning I would be summoned to her hearth, where she sat enthroned in a black waterfall of lace and silk, her skirts spilling across my feet. I stood to attention as she thundered at me her volleys of heroic verse and threatened me with hellfire. The stern evangelical Epp is the only one I remember, and I have written about her at greater length in my childhood memoir, *Hellfire and Herring*.

But there was another Epp, discovered years after she died – Epp the writer and recorder, the author of eccentric, erudite and outspoken journals and diaries; Epp the free spirit who travelled well beyond the humble confines of her east coast Scottish fishing village home, St Monans, where all our ancestors were born; and this is the Epp whom I am proud to present in this, the first of her 'notebooks'.

Epp's life would fill a novel: her seafaring ancestry, the great-grandfather who distinguished himself at Trafalgar, her humble upbringing and restricted education, her days as a chambermaid, followed by an affair with an aristocrat, a pregnancy, a sojourn in Paris, a return to Scotland and a childless marriage (possibly of convenience), and a dismal end as an employee in the village Post Office. Neither her family nor community were aware, it seems, of the remarkable calibre of mind of the woman who spent much of her life penning a remarkable series of Notes.

These Notes were never intended for publication but were written either for a particular young lady (a lost daughter?) or for women in general, or both. Either way she was clearly writing to express herself to herself, as writers do, and in so doing has achieved a universal audience.

Part manual, part journal, part commonplace book, Epp's guide touches on big universal topics (religion, evolution, ethical issues) and the nuts and bolts of living (food, health, sex), while she urges you to keep your mind and your bowels open, many of her views being staggeringly frank for her repressed and obscure time and place. It is a book about how to live and about the ultimate meaning of the life you live. It is also about being yourself and ignoring the exigencies of sex and class, the teachings of church and state. It is in fact a triumphant existential document, surpassing feminism, or any movement or trend.

While a few of the entries are adapted from eighteenth- and nineteenth-century sources, the spelling sometimes unchanged, most of them spring straight from her original and inquiring mind, offering an engagingly encyclopaedic take on life, a quirky and quixotic *Enquire Within*, all of her own. The span is also phenomenal: she was reading right up to her death, while some of the references point to a time when Tennyson was still alive, and she records thoughts on Darwin of which Professor Richard Dawkins might take note. It is a refreshingly relevant record of one woman's response to life, and is a sheer delight to read.

Christopher Rush

A Cure For a Sore Throat, Dr Robinson's

Take two dozen or thirty leaves of sage, pour over them a pint of boiling water, and let the infusion stand for half an hour. Add vinegar and honey to taste. It is the combination of the stringent and the emollient principle which works the desired effect: indeed it seldom fails. Gargle with this four times a day. Many gargles are unpleasant to the taste, but this one may be swallowed not only without danger, but with advantage.

A Good Basic Coq Au Vin

Your traditional cockerel is two-and-a-half times the size of the hen and takes four or five times longer to cook. Observe the following procedure: bacon diced; shallots peeled and halved; whole garlic cloves unpeeled; bouquet garni (bay, rosemary, thyme); two bottles of Beaujolais; and your cockerel, with breasts and legs off. Flour the joints, sear them in a nice big pan, and fry the vegetables six minutes; then take them out, put in two glasses of wine, and scrape well the bottom of the pan to salvage the flavoursome scraps. Reduce the liquid by half the quantity, throw all back in, cover with the rest of the wine, and simmer for six hours. In such a dish your cock will all but crow.

A Good Sick Drink

To one quart of boiling water add ½ oz sugar-candy, ¼ oz cream of tartar, and a handful of lemon and orange chips combined. When cold pour off.

A Jugged Hare

Fillet it and put it into water for two or three hours; take it out & cutt it into small pieces; season it with beaten mace, nutmeg, pepper & salt; put it into a pot, tye it down close; set it into a boiler of water; boyl it three hours then take your soss pan & burn a quarter of a lb of butter; put in your hare & gravy with half a juse of lemon. Sieve it a little and serve it hot.

A Liquor To Wash Old Deeds

This may be used on old paper or parchment when the writing has been obliterated, or when sunk, to make it legible again.

You need:
  5 or 6 galls
  1 pint strong white wine

Bruise the galls and drop them into the wine, which must stand in the sun for two days, so have an eye to the weather when you prepare this remedy. Take a clean or new artist's paintbrush, dip it into the wine, and wash that part of the manuscript on which the writing has sunk; and by the colour you will find whether it be strong enough of the galls. This is Mrs Rundell's receipt of 1868, she being too decorous a lady in her domestic advice to acquaint you with the information that your own urine will do as well as the wine, if not better. So pee a pint and drink the wine.

A Receipt

Take a quarter of a pound of raisins of ye Sun, half a pound of figs, 2 quarts of Liquorice, 1 oz of Aniseed. Stone the raisins, slice the figs & Liquorice; boil all these in 2 quarts of spring water till a pint be wasted. Drink a Chocolate Cupful the first thing in the morning and last at night for a Month or Six Weeks.

A Roman Pie

When the wind's up and the wood's in trouble, Mr Housman sits down and writes a poem. The Roman would have made a pie, and this is how it would have been:

½ lb pastry
mixed cooked spring vegetables, such as some young carrots,
   early potatoes and some tomatoes
a little cooked macaroni or spaghetti
seasoning
half a cup of rich brown gravy
one chopped chive and a little chopped parsley

Now line a cake tin with pastry and make a round lid to fit it. Bake the pastry in the tin and the pastry lid separately. When the vegetables are tender but still quite firm, add them to the gravy, macaroni, and the seasoning. Fill the cooked pie with the mixture, put on the lid, heat for a few minutes in the oven. Turn out upside down to serve, and surround with a border of spinach to conceal the little gravy that will leak out where the lid was fixed on. Eat your fill, and find out how the Roman felt on Wenlock Edge.

Today the Roman and his trouble
Are ashes under Uricon.

The tree of man was never quiet, but this simple little pie will quieten him in the worst of storms.

A Very Laxative Jam

For those chronic cases in the very bowels of hell, here is a laxative jam to unjam the party's part, and break the blockade in the sweetest possible manner. For your assault and battery on the stubborn bowel, you need to mince up and soak overnight:

1 lb of prunes
1 lb of raisins
¼ lb of blanched almonds, chopped

As soon as the sun has risen on the following day you should add 1 lb of demerara sugar and gently boil for half an hour, then pot and seal without delay, to close in the sweetness and strength. Give to the party in his porridge as generously as you like. All hell will break loose, but he will quickly be in the bowels of Christ.

A Wine Roll

Soak a penny French roll in raisin wine till it is a proper sop and will hold no more. Place it in the dish and round it pour a good custard, or cream, lemon juice and sugar. Just before it is served sprinkle it with nonpareil comfits, or stick it round with some blanched slit almonds. This is a glorious sop, and one that goes down sweetly.

Abstinence

Abstinence makes the heart grow fonder and so the greatest sybarite and the jolliest *bon viveur* will know the virtue of abstinence in adding to the renewed pleasure of what he has denied himself. After any prolonged period such as Lent, the rediscovered joy of indulgence will be immensely enhanced, may even prove overwhelming. To abstain, therefore, from a loved pleasure is mere commonsense, as custom stales the appetite.

It is all too easy on the other hand to make a sin of abstinence. To do without simply for the supposed inherent virtue of doing without is contrary to scripture as well as sense. God made the world and he saw that it was 'good'. The ascetics were mistaken when they supposed that earthly things were inferior to heavenly, material to spiritual. There are different levels of good, that is all, and the true virtue is not abstinence but temperance; whereas constant self denial, especially of matter, and of fleshly pleasures, is unhealthy, inhibits experience and is a crime against life.

Aches and Pains

Make a marinade out of half a dozen big heads of garlic and a pint of brandy, and keep it to hand. Drink a teaspoon of this as soon as you wake and immediately after your quick cold bath. This is a good way to oil yourself into the day and is a great remedy for ancient or aching bones. Once you have gone the way of all the earth, your brandied and be-garlicked bones will do the earth a power of good, and you will be at peace together.

Action

Action is momentary, the movement of a muscle, this way or that. Suffering is long, obscure and infinite. Consider this before you undertake or commit *any* action.

Actresses

Their silk stockings and white bosoms excited the amorous propensities even of the scholarly Dr Johnson, but you need neither silk stockings nor a white bosom to be an actress. Your hose can be worsted and your breast burnt by the sun. You do not even require a stage, or a play, for the world's one, and life's one, and you are the player. All men are your audience, and if you are fortunate, one man in particular. For him you must act well, playing out the part life has assigned to you: to entice, enchant, enfold, and enjoy constant attention, admiration and applause.

Adultery

What men call gallantry and gods adultery
Is much more common where the climate's sultry.

As Byron well knew, therefore, adultery is best committed abroad, though not too far east, where they would stone you for a wink. The further east you go, the lower you fall in the rank and file of creation. There a man may be as promiscuous as a monkey but a woman must be chaste as ice. Italy and Spain are splendid places for the fickle, but France is the bed and birthplace of inconstancy. There, if your man proves untrue to you and you stab him in the heart, they will accord you a public accolade and hang garlands round your neck. In England they will hang you *by* the neck.

It is worth remembering that every man is an adulterer, since according to Christ, 'He that looketh on a woman to lust after her hath committed adultery with her already, in his heart.' And since the man does not live who has not lusted after a woman, every man is an offender. The same is not true for you, whom nature has made so much more selective of men. There is nothing wrong with adultery if marriage is a torture chamber or a desert. All commandments were made to be broken.

Is adultery a sin? No. The Seventh Commandment forbids what is simply the physical expression of a perfectly natural desire, inhibited by society, and by the church, which is society's screw to keep you in your place, especially if you are a woman, and it is these two institutions (for society, too, is an institution) which have set up centuries of artificial barriers to human happiness.

Advice for Life

Always keep an open mind and open bowels. Close the one and you become a bore: close both and you become a dead bore. And nobody will be listening to you any more. The bowels need roughage: eat porridge in the morning, and always eat your potatoes in their jackets. The mind needs roughage too: do not over-sweeten it with romantic novels, but cram in hard fact. Most of it your brain will expel, as the bowels expel the oats and potatoes.

Read Shakespeare, the Bible, Mr Tennyson, and the marvellous Miss Dickinson. And never be in a hurry. Why indeed should you hurry, when every way you fly, you are molested equally by immortality? It will come to you in time. So let it come when it will. And eat, think and live well. Then you will die well too.

Age

There is nothing new under the sun, we are told. So your recorded age is irrelevant. You may be seventy and stupid, sixteen and sage. Your true age is unfathomable, as you have been here before and will return again. This is what Solomon meant when he spoke of there being no new thing under the sun. You may be a thousand years old, or ten thousand, it doesn't matter. What really matters is not how old but how wise you've grown, how far you have evolved, and what you have learned. The great affair is to avoid stagnation, and keep on the move.

Do not waste one second of your present span, which is short, worrying about your age. If you think you are old, you are wrong. You have been evolving for thousands of years, and when did you ever grow less by dying? Death is another step forward for you; and as you have progressed from insect to animal to human being, so you will go on to become a better and better human being. There is no end to your age, or to your life, and there is no such thing as death, there are only deaths.

Alcohol, Effects of, Excess of, and How to Cure

Toast well a slice of fine stale bread so that it be completely browned all over. Place in a jug and cover with boiling water, then cover with a saucer and allow to cool. It will prove peculiarly grateful to the stomach and easily carries off the effects of excess of drinking.

Cures other than toast:

Prevention: either by total abstinence (not recommended); by not drinking to excess in the first place (easier than abstinence but easily scuppered in one's cups); or by forestalling the evil effects once you have over-indulged by consuming a quantity of water equal to the amount of alcohol you have consumed. This may not save you entirely but will greatly alleviate the inevitable distress.

Palliation: of which there are many remedies. Freshly squeezed orange juice in large quantities; a breakfast of porridge followed by eggs and bacon; or, if you cannot countenance food, the infallible egg nog. Break two eggs into a bowl, add some milk and sugar according to instinct (self-preservation) and a handsome sip of brandy. Whisk well and consume quickly. Any hair of the dog will always help in whatever form you take it. The Romans swore by owls' eggs, advised by the Elder Pliny, who stole the idea from the Egyptians. But whatever night-thief would steal an owl's eggs for the relief of his own just deserts in drinking, deserves to be visited himself by the thief in the night (Revelation 3:3) and put to silence.

Alder

The old folk advised you never to cut the alder, whose sap runs like blood, but the alder shed more blood than the yew and elm and poplar put together that made the old English bows and arrows, and made short work of the French, for the alder made the best gunpowder, so fine that it increased the range of the cannon on the men-o'-war easily by a hundred, and some reckoned by nearly two hundred feet. The leaves infused make an excellent tea for the dropsy. When cooled, apply to the temples to soothe the fevered brain, or to the feet, for tired and aching soles; and weary souls will feel the difference too. An old remedy is to slip an alder leaf into either shoe before setting out on a long journey. The old ones believed that the tree spirits would keep you safe and well, and there is little wrong with that belief, but there is no doubt that the action of the feet on the leaves released the properties that made the traveller feel better, and therefore blessed.

Alexander

This herb affords you free celery, though it is known as the horse-parsley and the wild parsley for you will find it growing freely along the sunny seacoasts in summer, and the stalks are as tasty as any celery in a sandwich, and good to add to vegetable broth. It helps to break wind, to expel the afterbirth; and both seeds and stalks will help you to pee, and promote your periods, provoking both where there is obstruction. As they say, if the red flag is late in flying, Alexander will run it up the pole for you in no time, and is worth the salute for peace of mind. You worry that you may be with child, and anxiety makes you late, and later still; but a little of this herb in your salads and you will not be mooning about your monthlies any more. In short, it has many of the virtues of the common parsley, and the seed was sold in the old days for Macedonian parsley-seed, hence *Petroselinon Macedonicum*. It goes extremely well with fish.

An Easy Cheese Dish

Take two Spanish onions, quite large. Peel, cut and boil them up until soft. Then chop them small, almost minced. Now add some grated cheese such as cheddar. Into the pan put a couple of good knobs of butter and a breakfast cupful of cream, not too runny. Stir well, simmer for a very little while, and serve up on good hot thick buttered toast.

An Easy Vomit

Two large teaspoonfuls of ready-made mustard in a quarter of a pint of warm water, working it off with weak Chamomile tea.

For a Sick Stomach, Salt put in weak Chamomile tea is often an effectual vomit.

Anaemia

If you are overcome by a perpetual daily feeling of intense weariness, pervading your entire system, it is possible you may be anaemic. Examine yourself in the mirror: are your eyes dull? Is your complexion white? Pull down the skin just below your lower eyelashes, and look at the flesh underneath the eye: has it lost its healthy redness? Do your fingernails tell the same story? Are your monthly flows excessive, and do you feel particularly fatigued around the time of your periods? Certainly you should eat lots of lentils and beans, with spinach and watercress for salads. You should also try Wincarnis for speedy relief. It is the wine of life and you may send for a liberal free trial bottle to Coleman & Co., Ltd., WI33, Wincarnis Works, Norwich. It is no mere taste but enough to make you feel better, and the only requirement is to enclose three penny stamps to pay the postage.

Angelica

Angelica Archangelica flowers in early spring. An infusion of the leaves, fresh or dried, or water distilled from the root, will rid you of wind, or the painful effects of a cold. Drunk thus it will help you pee, and the juice, dropped into mouth, ears or eyes, will cure toothache, deafness and dimness of sight. You may use it for salads, fruit salads, sandwiches and cakes. When the stems are candied it is also good for the belly, relieving stomach upsets and pains.

Dose:
of the powdered root, 10–20 grains
distilled water, 1 ounce
extract, 5–15 grains
infusion, 1 tablespoonful or more
tincture, 1 drachm
spirits, ½ drachm – 3 drachms

Angelica Cordial: take a small handful of the angelica stems, stripped of the leaves, and the threads picked out, then cut into small pieces. To 1 lb put 12 pints of brandy, or more; 2 drachms of cinnamon, 1 of mace, with 12 cloves; dissolve 4 lbs of sugar in 6 pints of water, and mix all in a well-stopped jar. Let it stand thus for six weeks, then filter and bottle for use. This is Dr Robinson's receipt, which is most serviceable in windy complaints.

Angels

Only an idiot would doubt their existence, or the certainty that they existed at one time, for there are too many examples of their appearances to be ignored. In biblical times, they materialised at important moments and announced matters of consequence. The real question is: what were these angels?

The Greeks called them angels simply because they were messengers. By this token your postman may be an angel, especially when he arrives bearing a *billet-doux*. Then you may kiss his feet and go no further. Your milkman is liable to prove less angelic, with his fingers ever in the udders, and his feet of cowshed clay, and not to be kissed.

The old scholars and artists gave them wings simply because they imagined that they had travelled to earth through the cosmos and obviously required the powers of flight similar to birds. In all probability they were humans of superior ability, because Genesis describes them as the sons of God. You are also told that they looked on the daughters of men and went in unto them, and so a superior strain was unquestionably developed on earth. This strain became diluted over time, which is why 'angels' no longer appear, and beings such as Jesus and Socrates and Shakespeare and Michelangelo are no longer possible, only artists and scientists who play and tinker, but have lost touch with greatness because they have lost touch with the divine in man.

Angels on Horseback

If you have a dozen descended on you for a tasty breakfast and you need twelve legions of angels summoned to your side, this is what to do. Take as many slices of bacon, roll up, take an oyster for each slice, skewer on the roll, and do this twelve times, or until you have a full ashet. Bake for half an hour or until ready, and out of the oven come your angels on horseback, to make your guests sing your praises. They will also serve as a fine supper.

Animals

Innocence and instinct are the lot of the animals. They know no sin, nor can they commit sin. It is grossly wrong, therefore, to liken evil, brutal, or even slovenly human beings to animals. This is an insult to the beasts, which God made innocent, and though they have no souls, they have spirits, many a beast being better spirited than many a man or woman. Animals kill by instinct and not for creed, greed, malice, cruelty or sport. Always be kind to these dumb friends; where they must be killed, see that it is done quickly and humanely; and while they are with you, always feed them and settle them first, serving them before yourself, as any countryman or woman well knows.

Remember too that they are your brothers and sisters, and that while they must be killed for food, no creature should be harmed that is not pestiferous. Those who hurt them and use deliberate and gratuitous cruelty should not be hanged, but should be served in the same way as Jesus says you should treat those who harm children: 'Woe unto him who offends one of these little ones! It were better for that man that a millstone were hanged about his neck, and that he were cast into the depths of the sea.' This would be a just punishment for the wretch who drowns a sackful of kittens.

Aphrodisiacs

These are many and well known, but above all else men are unconsciously attracted by the vaginal scents, which are naturally mingled with lingering urinal aromas, not at all unpleasant if recent, assuming older odours washed off by process of personal hygiene. It is to defeat the purpose to add your own urine to the food, only to mask it with strong flavours. You will use only a very small amount, so small as not to affect the taste but to attract unconsciously by scent. This should be added superficially, sparingly, and last. You may also dab a handkerchief appropriately and equally delicately and keep it about you. Males are aware of this but *not* aware, and have been known to go mad with longing. Never tell this secret, however, as the knowledge itself empowers you and imparts a natural authority which a man cannot resist.

Apples

Put them in puddings, pancakes, pastries and pies; batter them, dumple them, fritter or fry; make an omelette, a Charlotte, or simply turn them out baked to sweeten a sharp tooth. An apple on the table will never cause discord and will make you the apple of the eater's eye. Crush them into cider and he will drink from no cup but yours and will love you like Solomon. After that the lovesick man is yours for life. Eve gave the apple a bad name as the cause of the Fall. But the fall of an apple is Paradise Regained, however you cook it.

Archangel

The archangels are red, white and yellow, also known to the old folk as dead nettle and bee nettle. They stop the whites in women; take it if you have the discharge. For this you should use the white archangel, according to the signatures. It heals green wounds, bruises and burns, and is a greatly exhilarating herb, driving away melancholy and making your heart merry, like wine in winter at the ribs of the fire.

25

Ash

The leaves should be gathered in June, and are excellent for arthritis and folk with rheumatism. Once gathered, they should be very well dried, powdered down, and stoppered close in very well-corked bottles. The ash key prevails against the fart, but provokes urine, and the ash keys you may keep all year, and use them in winter when you cannot get the leaves. But you may always use the bark instead, the ashes of which, made into a ley, may be rubbed into scabbed and leprous heads, and give them an excellent cleansing.

Asthma

For asthma or Difficulty in Breathing, take a teaspoonful of white mustard seed bruised, mixt in treacle & at night, going to bed.

Asthmatics

You need to get a good ounce of liquorice stick from the chemist, cut it up and keep it steeping for a whole day and entire night in a couple of pints of water, stirring occasionally. You should keep this bottled and ready to be drunk whenever the sufferer has need of it. Or you can slice up some apples, which should then be boiled and the water strained off. A good draught of this and he will breathe the easier. It is also pleasant for the breath, especially the liquorice.

Atheism

An atheist is a fool, not because he does not believe in God, but because he has a closed mind. Any shut mind is a fool's mind. Shun the company of such fools, avoid all contact with them, for they preach from the pulpits of their own convictions, and nothing kills a man as dead as conviction. If you are a true woman you will have fewer and flimsier convictions, for conviction is masculine, ambiguity feminine, and intuition is the road ahead. The atheist has no intuition; he leads you up a blind alley. As for the agnostic, drink with him and gabble with him all night long, for there lives more faith in honest doubt, believe me, than in half the creeds, and there is no creed so absolute as atheism.

Austen, Effects of Jane Austen on Intelligent Adults

You can tell from Miss Austen's letters to her sister Cassandra and others, new published, why she could never be a great writer. At the height of the Napoleonic Wars she writes: 'We do not lack amusements. Bilbocatch, spillikins, paper ships, riddles, conundrums and cards, with watching the flow and ebb of the river, and now and then a stroll out, keep us well employed.'

Well employed! And spillikins – when men were spilling out their lives on the battlefields of Europe. You may argue that she sensibly wrote of what she knew. But herein lies the trouble. What she knew was social man, and therefore superficial man. Compare her situation, for example, with Shakespeare's. He knew more of life, certainly; but did not know (presumably) what it was like to be a murderer, a regicide, a rapist; to be a black man in white society, or an older man married to a younger woman. In his case it was the reverse of the last that was true.

And yet it is Shakespeare who explores such situations with the instinctive art of the truly great writer, who does not require experience in order to examine experience but allows imagination to do the business for him.

Miss Austen is devoid of imagination, for she writes with her head, not from her soul, and from the relatively undisturbed routines of her family life. In this she is elegant, ironic and witty, writing excellent English, and the best that may be said of her in these regards is that she is so much better than the tedious Mrs Gaskell. But this is not enough. The best advice would be to spend your precious hours on neither, but to read the Brontës, who were considerably more confined than Miss Austen, but emancipated themselves by their imaginations, Emily especially, whereas J. A. merely played at living, as huge events raged around her and the greatest man in Europe stood just across the Channel while she played spillikins and wrote about the concerns of bored aristocrats.

Miss Austen is greatly suited to intelligent Adolescents, who admire the poise and perfection of her language and aspire to emulate it. Other than the language, there is some irony, and witty observation of a tiresome stratum of society. As soon as you outgrow your adolescence you will outgrow Miss Austen, for what sort of a writer leaves an intelligent adult entirely unruffled? Our Scotsmen have dismissed her books as dishwashings; our full-blooded American brothers have found her sterile and repugnant; and the more than full-blooded Mr Lawrence was nauseated by what he termed a narrow-gutted spinster, lacking in class and character.

It is not sex that is in question here; nor politics; nor rivalry between writers of different sexes or classes. Even the glorious Charlotte remarks that Miss Austen is unacquainted with the stormy sisterhood, by which she means the passions. No female in Miss Austen's novels feels for a man the way Jane does for Mr Rochester, or for that matter he for her. No woman who has never opened her legs to a man, or for that matter to a woman, can presume to open her mind to life.

As to the facts, we will doubtless never know them. That Miss Austen died untried by a man is more than likely; that she died entirely untried by a woman is a little less likely. That she herself had passions is unquestionable: she was a human being; but that she leaves no record of these passions in her books is unforgivable. No reader will emerge from Jane Austen's novels a changed human being; they will not make you more human than you already are; and in this she misses the entire point of literature.

Bad Breath

This can arise either from inefficient teeth-brushing or from acid in the stomach, sometimes caused by nerves. A glass of warm water before and after bed is good for the stomach. Wash out your mouth with carbolic acid in a little warm water. After that chew some liquorice to mask the medicinal smell. Or mix the acid with rosewater, to which you have added a teaspoon each of tinctures of calamus and orrisroot and some spirit of nutmeg.

If the bad breath is caused by tobacco you need one teaspoon of tincture of myrrh and half a teaspoon of spirits of camphor in one pint of hot water and a little borax. You should then use this mixture when brushing your teeth, as toothpaste alone will not eradicate the problem.

Bad breath may however prove a most powerful contraceptive against the ardour of the most rampant male, and if you have a good reason to wish him kept at bay, then smile on him horribly, and if he is hot for you, give him a bitch's kiss and under your dogbreath watch his ardour wane.

Baldness

To cure a man's hairlessness the best treatment is the least liked by the bald party. You must obtain fresh henshit at the end of each day; heat it just enough, but not so as to dry it out, and spread it on a rag, which should then be clapped hard onto the bald patch, or the entire pate, and kept there for as long as possible. Place an old cap on the head to keep the poultice in place during the hours of sleep. It may be kept there during the working day, but remind him, if he is a courteous gentleman, not to doff his cap to a lady. This should go on for six months, and during the following six months the hair will begin to sprout again.

Henshit gathered in spring and early summer is the most effective. Winter henshit is dour and will not tempt the follicles back into life nearly so effectually. This is a deep treatment that demands time, and a patience that men as a species often lack. And few women will sleep for half a year with a head of henshit on the adjoining pillow. But if both can stand it, the man may emerge as Absolom and with the curls and vigour of a ram. Samson regained his strength with his restored hair, which may be attributable to nothing more than regained self-respect. But a bald man may prove perfectly potent between the sheets, and even more so, given that his energies are not dissipated in worrying over his looks. And you need have little care what he looks like when the lights are out, even if there are no locks to hold onto.

Baptism

It is said that if an infant fails to cry at its baptism, even when it feels the cold water, it is unlikely to live long. This is superstition, but to be on the safe side keep a small pin between your finger and thumb, and at the moment of wetting the head, if the infant still does not cry, then give it a good prick to make sure it does. A good bawling lets out the body's stress and the tightness from the soul, even in infants, and is good for general health.

If you can give the infant something made of coral, a bauble, or just a small fragment of coral to hang round the neck at baptism, this will help later with the cutting of the teeth, and later still will help to fix the teeth in the mouth, all the more so in men, and to keep them there, good and firm.

Bay

Its scent has been known to bring dead men back to life, or so the story goes. Certainly the old story testifies to its piercing fragrance, which is one excellent reason why you should plant one near the door of the house, and more so because the sweet scent of life drives back the dark ones, that thrive on corruption and stink. Old Nick himself cannot abide the scent of the bay. Put a bay leaf into your pillow and you may see in sleep the likeness of the one whom you will marry. At the very least you will dream true dreams.

Beach, The

The beach is a great book, which you should read; it is no mere playground for children, or for a promenade. You can find trees hundreds of millions of years old in the rocks. You can see whinstone blocks with the scores of the ice-age glaciers on them, a mere 20,000 years old. It is a fascinating story to be read in pages of stone. But only the fool believes that this great book contradicts that other great book, the Bible. Mr Lyell and Mr Darwin never thought to attack that book, or the Book of Genesis: on the contrary they drew your attention to the wonders of creation, and so to the power and majesty of the Creator, applauded by Mr Darwin at the conclusion of his sublime work *On the Origin of Species by Means of Natural Selection*:

There is grandeur in this view of life, with its several powers, having been originally breathed by the Creator into a few forms or into one; and that, whilst this planet has gone cycling on according to the fixed law of gravity, from so simple a beginning endless forms most beautiful and most wonderful have been, are being evolved.

Sadly there are those who, wishing for their own reasons to attack religion, have used Darwin as their mouthpiece, and this is an insult not so much to God (in whom they are entitled, after all, not to believe) as to a great scientist, whose work and reputation they ignorantly or shamelessly pervert. Only later did Darwin harden his heart against God, but it was not evolution that killed his belief, but the death of his beloved daughter, and it was not the *Origin of Species* that turned his face from the church, but the church's own damnable doctrines which have nothing to do with God. If you wish to read God's Word go not to the church but to the shore, and you will read in the stones and hear from the sea what He has to say.

Beat Time in Winter, To

Some folk rise later in winter, but as the days grow shorter you must rise the earlier to make greater use of the restricted amount of daylight available to you. Use the darkness for work that does not require full light, but as soon as dawn breaks see to those tasks where greater precision of sight is required, so that when night falls early you are not hurrying about the house with lit candles. You can tell late risers by the candle-grease stains on their floors and furnishings and other surfaces; and of course they run the greater risk of fire.

Bed, To Ensure Proper Airing

Fresh air is the best method and nothing beats a bed that has come in straight from the fresh air, with the winds in it, and the scents of grasses. If the mattress is not outside ensure that all windows are well open, with a good draught pouring through the room. Then make up and use the warming pan. As soon as the pan is removed, take a small clear glass or tumbler and set it between the sheets. If the bed has been properly aired the glass will go cloudy and that is all. But if the bed be not sufficiently dry, drops will appear on the glass, resulting from the continuing dampness of the bed, which should on no account be slept in.

Bedwetting

Sew a tiny pocket to the back of the nightshirt, nightdress, or pyjamas, insert a small pebble, clothes-peg, bobbin or cotton-reel, and sew up the opening to prevent the object from falling out. The bedwetter will unconsciously avoid sleeping on the back and will be the less prone to the condition. Never scold a child for this, and on no account strike the child. Hard words, especially if accompanied by beating, will merely create anxiety, the stress of which will not alleviate but aggravate the problem. Nature will soon iron out what is nature's expression of some hidden trouble. But this simple trick should work. It will not work if your bedwetter is an old person. Incontinence is another matter. If your bedwetter is a grown person but not advanced in years, the remedy is still effective. In some men it is an alcoholic problem: stop the drinking and you stop the pee-the-bed. If he cannot refrain from the bottle, tie a bag of fresh dandelions round his neck, if they be in flower. If not, use dried, from your store of herbs, but fresh is better, and one pee-the-bed helps another to wake and do the business.

Bees

Pigmy seraphs gone astray,
Velvet people from Vevay,
Belles from some lost summer day,
Bees' exclusive coterie.

So writes Miss Dickinson of the humble bumblebee, inebriate of air and debauchee of dew. When you see him drunk with pollen, droning low over the fields, enter his essence, his essential alcoholism; envy and admire him, as saints and seraphs do when they see the little tippler leaning against the sun.

These little tipplers, these velvet folk from Vevay, are sensitive creatures and feel keenly the passing away of the beekeeper, if he has kept the hives for any length of time. If such a one dies, therefore, or is at the point of death, be ready to turn the hives the other way, or to move them quickly to another part of the garden. Do this again when the coffin is borne away, for there have been many instances of all the bees dying in the hives at the very moment, or soon afterwards, of the keeper's death, or at the death of the master; and again this mass death may occur when the master takes his final departure. He leaves the house, the swarm senses the sudden void, and the pigmy seraphs give up the ghost, down to the last single bee. It has been noted that turning the hives, if carried out in time, may prove an antidote to this mass destruction. Death is bitter enough, but to add to it the loss of so much sweetness is even worse.

Betrayal

Who would be a traitor knave? Who would fill a coward's grave? To betray your husband is one thing. Most husbands would sell you for a shilling; it is in the nature of men, and you may do as you are done unto. But never betray your friends or your country. The worst treachery is to your own person, to desert your better self and be untrue to your heart; and a love that once was a thing of truth and beauty − not a social contract − has become like the rose in William Blake's poem:

O rose, thou art sick!
The invisible worm
That flies in the night
In the howling storm

Has found out thy bed
Of crimson joy,
And his dark secret love
Does thy life destroy.

Stolen waters are sweet, and bread eaten in secret is pleasant, but the dark secret love that destroys the rose is satanic. It is the Judas kiss. You will often receive it, even second hand, for such kisses are blown about the world. Never give it. Or if you do, you have an appointment with an elder tree.

Blackthorn Winter

This is a prolonged winter and a cruel one, with freezing east sea-winds wailing round the gable ends all through March and well into April, and the blackthorns blooming amid sleet and snow. Keep children indoors during a blackthorn winter, when the cold will get into their bones at once and they may catch their death.

Bladder

Use a strong infusion of clivers for any urinary obstructions. You will find this goose grass in hedges and ditches, flowering in early summer, and though it is injurious to whatever grows near it, the juice of the herb is affectionate to all orifices, particularly for earache, uterus, gravelly complaints, the bloody flux, the removal of slimy matter from kidneys and bladder, and the speedy removal of suppressed urine.

Bleeding, To Stop

A cobweb is the oldest cure, and nature's way, as the wise old owl knew very well when he bandaged the little grey rabbit's bleeding stump with one, having bitten off her nice white tail, which he wanted for a door knocker. That is why owls are so wise. When you apply a cobweb it will staunch the blood, provided the wound be not too deep. In such a case, do not be in such a hurry to clear the cobwebs from your corners. Cobwebs are curative too, and catch the flies. You may also sprinkle flour on the cut, or use Hazeline.

Bloody Flux

This is distressingly common, especially among children, and while the child is being carried through the necessary and correct course of medicine, give the child chicken broth, and afterwards a little brandy and loaf sugar burned together, and a strong tea of poplar bark.

Blushing

This is becoming enough in a virgin, but if you burst into flame, face, neck and breast at the slightest word, you may look more like a methylate than a maid, and your maidenly blushes render you unsightly as a sot. Use gentian compound, infusion of, a very small glass of it, morning and evening. Otherwise, when a man pays you a compliment and finds himself looking at a beetroot, he will quickly retract, and you will remain a maid. The gentian itself will not lose you your virginity but your blushes will be lost, or at least subdued. Alternatively, this miserable habit may be permanently cured by Taylor & Co., Dept D., 149 Fleet Street, London. The cure is harmless and inexpensive, and the remedy may be sent for privately, under cover, for two penny stamps.

Body, The

If your body be a temple, as the Bible says, then be sure to admit only those who will worship there, and especially those who first remove their shoes, as even the infidels have the grace to do.

Body Odour

All the spices of Arabia will not sweeten your person if not properly washed. If you tend to exude odours you should make good use of coal tar or carbolic soaps. They may not be equal to Araby, but the scent of soap is to be preferred to that of your armpits or your feet; powder will simply supply you with a scented stink, and you will live a barren sister all your life, all your womanly charms lost on man, whose nostrils you offend. If your condition is extreme you need to dust yourself down with boracic acid powder and apply it to your shoes and stockings in good measure. You will not smell like Cleopatra but folk will not fly when they spy you coming, and the mice may return to your wainscot.

Boils

These may be the result of underfeeding, overfeeding or wrongful feeding. Eat rhubarb, fish, milk and eggs, and get plenty of cod liver oil into you. Otherwise if you be prone to them, the boils will rain down on you as they did on Job, or on those old Egyptians when God was punishing Pharaoh. If you have the boils already, take some fresh yeast to stop more coming, for like Claudius's sorrows, they come not single spies but in battalions. Add a speck of sulphate of calcium from the chemist.

For immediate application you should make a poultice of chamomile flowers, or haricot beans powdered, mixed with fenugreek and honey; also applications of tinctures of iodine, camphor, carbolic, solution of caustic, glycerine or belladonna. Bathe constantly with cotton wool soaked in water as hot as you can stand it and hotter, till you howl like old Nebuchadnezzar when he was a wolf. This will speed the boil to the bursting point, after which apply antiseptic, and afterwards lay on lint spread with this. Never lay dry lint too quickly on a burst boil. It will stick to the sore and will prove the devil's own job to remove without breaking the scab.

A snail is a sure cure. The true virtue of the snail sits in its slime, which contains nature's medicine. If a boil has come to the point where it will neither come to a head and burst, nor die down and leave you in peace, take from the fields or garden the largest snail you can find, and put him on the sore place. You will find that the clever little creature will not retreat into his shell but will come out all the more to meet the swelling, and will readily allow you to use him to the purpose, which is to rub him slowly and gently into the afflicted area. The juice will gather and flow and the boil will drink it up. Repeat the process every six hours but with a different snail, otherwise you kill the snail by extracting all the virtue out of him. Within a few hours of the first application you will find that the swelling will be much reduced and, instead of bursting, which is painful in itself and may cause subsequent infection, the head of the sore will simply begin to shrink, the angry hardness and flame will soften and cool, and within a day or so your boil will be no more. Within one week the skin will be as it was before, with never a blemish. Now place the snail back where you found him, and well away from the thrush. Who else would eat such a creature, or harm this humble country doctor? Only the frog, of course.

Bowels

White Pond Lily roots may be used if they are first well washed, split into strips, dried and pulverised, afterwards to be drunk as a tea. An infusion of chamomile will afford relief, as will wake-robin root, dried, powdered, and mixed with honey or syrup. A teaspoonful of candleberry sweetened in hot water will also work to relieve disorders of the bowels, besides being an excellent powder for teeth and gums, a clearer of heads and headaches, and a first-rate snuff.

43

Breasts

In time of singleness, courtship and love, they are your weapons of war, for while your other charms remain suitably draped and so hidden from men's eyes, your bosom, by its shape and contour, is always on show, and though your breasts themselves are not seen, they are in evidence by suggestion. You should take care to increase and encourage that suggestion by all means possible, short of décolletage. The latter should be restricted to certain company, select or private, custom having altered from the times when a bared bosom signified the maidenly rather than the matronly condition.

The power of breasts lies in men's fascination, and even reverence. This extends beyond courtship and marriage to procreation and the suckling of infants, when your breasts will acquire an even greater power over a man as symbols of your fertility and force of life. This is a mystery he can only wonder at, and it is in this elevated state of excitement that he wishes to be suckled. Allow him this liberty, for you are indeed Liberty breaking the barricades, and some men will confess to an experience in milking you far greater and more pleasurable even than the delights of intercourse itself.

Breasts That Are Hard and Swelled

If your breasts are so hard and enlarged as to be painful to all contact, an excellent remedy is to be made of chamomile flowers and marshmallow roots, bruised, of each one ounce, and boiled in one quart of water down to one pint. Bathe both breasts as hot as can be borne, then place the flowers and roots in a clean cloth and apply as a plaster or poultice.

Broom

You can make an infusion using the very highest tops of the early branches, and to a dozen teaspoonfuls of these, chopped small, put a pint and a half of spring water. This produces a magnificent spring tonic. For best results add an extra teaspoonful, making it up to thirteen, and take the water if you can from a north-flowing stream.

Bryony

In the case of the stillborn child give a decoction of root in wine; in the case of an obstructed menstrual flow take a drachm of the root in powder, mixed with white wine, and this will quickly bring it down; the roots, fruits and leaves are great skin cleansers, banishing all blemishes, and that is why the country folk used to call the berries tetter berries. They sometimes called the herb the wild vine or ladies' seal. The white vine bryony will cure constipation; the pessaries must be inserted well into the arse in order to prove effectual.

Bunions

Deadly nightshade is death to bunions, which dislike belladonna. Brush them with this and glycerine each day, which is an old remedy, or with iodine, more recent, which will nevertheless provide quick relief. This will also do well for carbuncles, though these are a more serious matter and require an internal attack to eradicate the cause. Plenty of good strengthening food is needed here, including mutton, raw eggs, and brandy. The brandy may be mixed with the egg, or if the sufferer is a child, slightly diluted with water.

Carpe Diem

There is nothing more to be said than these two words, though it has been said a thousand times in as many different ways: seize the day, gather ye rosebuds, eat drink and be merry, *Gaudeamus Igitur*, and, if you become a true fanatic of the philosophy, with all the zeal of the convert, *Meum est propositum in taberna mori*.

Catarrh

For all his ailments the great Dr Johnson never suffered from blocked tubes; and his secret was no secret at all: snuff. You can make your own from ground roasted coffee and sugar in equal quantities, crushed to a dust, and with just a touch of menthol. Or you may buy it in. They were great snuff-takers in the last century. Read Captain Gulliver's sea-travels, so real it is impossible they were invented. These big Brobdingnagian girls would strip bare naked in front of him, he being as small as a pet, and one even sat him astride one of her nipples, while he complained of their stink, and their cracked and hairy skins were awful to behold. But he never refers to catarrh, for they knew the value of snuff, even the ladies, and though their arses were unthinkable, their pipes were clear.

Cats

The cat is generally believed to be less loyal and less affectionate than the dog, a supposition arising from the false but plausible observation that the cat cares more for the house than for its occupants. The truth is that cats appear to cling to places rather than people precisely because they associate the place with the people who live there, and will stubbornly revisit a house whose occupant has died, or moved on, in the expectation of finding there the person to whom they are attached. Only after the person repeatedly fails to appear will the cat cease to haunt the house, but if she then happens to find the family who lived there, she will immediately attach herself as before, but in the new abode. There are many instances of this, as of cats covering considerable distances, even hundreds of miles, in their efforts to track down persons from whom they have been separated.

Change

Change and decay is the law of life. Death is the greatest change: for your body, it cannot be reversed, but for your soul, death is more than mere change, it is transition, and we shall all be changed. Diurnal change is mostly mundane. Did you change your stockings, your mind, your man, that book at the library? Is there to be a change of weather, of party, of Prime Minister? These are the trivialities that confront you, till death changes all. But never be afraid of change, if custom is killing you, for change can free you as surely as boredom puts you behind bars.

Chastity

There is much talk of this, and great expectation placed upon a woman, none on a man, no more than if you would expect a bee to produce milk, or a cow honey. That is very well for the man, who is not expected to comprehend the secret of chastity. As for you, understand one thing: chastity is a spiritual, or at least a mental condition, not a physical one. You are not to confuse it with virginity. There is no better representation of this in literature than Mr Hardy's Tess, who loses her virginity but remains chaste to the end. Many's the vile-minded virgin and chaste whore. *Splendide mendax et in omne virgo nobilis aevum.*

Chilblains

A simple remedy is to moisten the inside of a cucumber peel and lay it lightly on the place; it is not necessary to rub it in.

Or, if the chilblains have come with the cold snowy weather, rub them with snow from the fields. This is the remedy of a wise country doctor, the Little Grey Rabbit, who treated the Hare.

Or, get a little piece of alum and melt it down in a basin of water, in which you must plunge your hands for a full twenty minutes. Wear gloves when you go to bed. If there is one beside you, you may remove the gloves should you wish to be less formal, but wear them again when the informalities are over.

Or, mix early elderflowers with hog's lard; boil up and mix well; then strain and apply.

Or, boil up some celery stalks or walnut leaves, allow to cool and immerse your hands and feet in this for five minutes or more. If your feet are affected, wear good thick woollen socks in bed, taking them off as with the gloves, as occasion arises.

For a severe chilblain, remove an ember from the fire and place it in a tin; pee on it briefly, and while still hissing, pick it out of the tin with the tongs, and with it touch the chilblain lightly and fleetingly. Afterwards treat for a burn.

Childbirth

As soon as the baby is born, tie the umbilical with a piece of red cord, or strip of red flannel. If it is a boy, do not cut the umbilical cord too short, as the old folk said that the length left attached determines the length of the penis, and a man is best left too long than too short. If it is a girl, you should cut it short, as this will determine the length of her tongue, and you would do well by her to ensure that she does not turn into one of those long-tongued gossips, feared and eschewed by all.

Swaddle a newborn boy in his mother's petticoats, and if it is a girl, in her father's trousers or shirt, and this will protect the child against unwanted celibacy or childlessness in later life. This may be very likely an old wife's fable, but you will be wrapping the infant in something, and so the petticoats or shirt will do just as well, and will do no harm either, so you will lose nothing by observing the old custom.

Some say to put the newly born infant into a drawer, before the crib, and that this will ensure that the child is safe through life and secure from harm. Others say that the drawer prefigures the coffin, and that by doing this you will be putting him early to his grave. Both are old wives' tales, but the drawer is good for the reason that it is free from draughts.

Childbirth and Tides

If you are about to deliver when the tide is ebbing, use what means you may to retard the delivery. When the tide is going back is a dangerous time, which drains life and sets towards death; and a baby born when the tide is receding will always be in jeopardy of going back itself, or its spirits ebbing away. If the tide is flowing, bring on the baby as fast as you can. Floodtide increases life, ebbtide is death's door. This is no mere superstition of seafaring folk, for Sir John Falstaff slipped away with the tide, and the old writers were closer to nature than we are now.

Chimney Fire

Prevention being the best remedy, see to it that your lum is kept well swept and crept. It need be crept only once in a blue moon, but should be swept twice a year, oftener if your wood is damp, but you should take steps to ensure a dry log-pile, and so prevent the furring up of the flue. From time to time, send a goose up the chimney, which will provide a swift sweep, not so effective as the job done with brushes, but a good intermediate device and one that costs nothing.

If however a fire does break out in the chimney, you should throw up a good handful or two of salt, and also over the fire itself. If it continues to burn, two people may easily hold a blanket soaked in water over the opening of the chimney. Nails or knobs should be kept fixed in the ends of the mantelpiece so that if you are alone in the house during the chimney fire you may fasten the upper corners of the blanket there and hold the lower corners tight on either side of the grate. Swift action of this kind is what prevents chimney fires from spreading into much more serious affairs.

Clapshot

This is an easy nourishing dish, filling and flavoursome, if properly made. Cut up potatoes and turnips into small pieces, the turnip pieces smaller than the potatoes, and they should be in equal quantities. Some onions may be added and a little carrot, and some peeled garlic cloves. When boiled up and drained, everything should be mashed well together with two good knobs of butter, a good splash of milk, and plenty of salt and pepper. This dish is especially delicious if prepared immediately after the turnips have felt the first touch of frost in the fields, usually in late October or November.

Class

Consider the lies that will be laid on you in your lifetime. You will be instructed that the duty of the people under heaven is to serve and support the sovereign. That duty begins with your birth and can only end with your death, and during this time, which is your whole life, you must serve the needs of your king or queen, especially in time of war, which means that you will first be invited to fight for your sovereign under attack, and afterwards to pay the cost, on the assumption you have not paid already with your life.

The Bible preaches the doctrine of equality, which is an excellent doctrine, except that it is offensive to the pride and vanity of fallen man, and those in power have perverted it in order to justify their own position. It has been argued therefore that just as God created degrees of angels, so degrees of men; and the duty of the 'inferior' degrees is to serve, support and protect their 'superiors'. You will find this in the Westminster Confession of Faith, and in the Catechism. Do not be fooled by it, however, and do not be taken in by these old Divines. They were politicians got up in religious robes and, requiring the subservience of the majority, they invented a non-biblical system of law; they were the minority but they knew that a minority is always a majority if it has the power. Such were the officers of his or her Britannic Majesty.

And how to enforce this lie? By false religion. The Sixth Commandment orders you to honour your father and your mother. But who are your father and mother? 'By your father and mother are meant all those whom the Lord hath set in authority over you' – your social superiors. This is the monstrous perversion which has been preached for centuries, and which is nowhere to be found in the Bible, is not God's commandment, but is politics disguised as religion, and has provided those in office with false justification for wars and other injustices. The truth is that it is monarchy that is a false doctrine; it is offensive to nature and to reason; and there are no *classes* of men or of women, only such as have been invented by self-serving and time-serving liars. The only class to which you belong is the class of the individual, and in that class you are unique and beholden to none other.

Coffee

We know from the *Family Receipt Book* of 1820 that the infusion or decoction of the roasted seeds of the coffee berry, when not over strong, is a wholesome, exhilarating and strengthening beverage, and when mixed with a good proportion of milk, is a proper article of diet, especially for literary and sedentary people. Great minds do not always work with seated posteriors. Mozart composed at billiards, with his posterior stuck out, and Henry II of England saw to affairs of both stomach and state while on foot, being such an active and energetic monarch, with little time to dine. Neither were coffee drinkers, but it does improve the humour, is also good for the brains, and is especially suited to persons of advanced or advancing years. When drunk very strong it proves stimulating and heating in a considerable degree, producing thirst and watchfulness. It should not be drunk prior to sleep, as a rule, though some say the opposite, and that it sends them off into wonderfully active and useful dreams that cleanse the psyche. By an abusive indulgence in this drink the organs of digestion may be impaired, the appetite destroyed, nutrition impeded, and the more quickly brought on than otherwise would have occurred are: emaciation, general debility, paralytic affections and nervous fever. Note however that coffee corrects crudities, removes colic and flatulence; it cherishes the animal spirits, takes away listlessness and languor, and is serviceable in all obstructions arising from a languid circulation.

Colds, To Avoid

Some take a cold bath, but it is not necessary either to use up an amount of water as will fill the bath, or to immerse yourself entirely. An even better remedy is to sponge or splash yourself extremely vigorously with a good strong gush of cold water, throwing it over your head and shoulders and all parts of the body; but this must be done immediately on arising from bed, and should be followed at once by vigorous rubbing with a towel, which should be a little wetted. Afterwards you should use a dry towel and step into a dressing gown for a few minutes before putting on your clothes for the day. This entire operation will take up only five minutes of your day but will ensure that you are immediately awake and alert to the business of the day, that your skin is given a good tone; and the practice, if adopted daily without fail, while not providing the perfect guarantee that you will never catch a cold, as some have claimed, will certainly keep colds well at bay for most of your life.

Complexion

Slice up some cucumber, and either boil it or soak it in rum, then bathe your face with cotton wool well soaked in this. You may simply lie prone instead and keep the cucumber slices pressed directly to your face for some little time.

Or, warm up some milk fresh from the cow with violets mixed well in. The flowers must be freshly picked for this remedy. Or, use oatmeal, strained, adding bay rum to the liquor.

These are effective remedies for helping you to a soft white complexion, if you wish it, and to keep your face free from wrinkles.

If you suffer from excessive dryness or greasiness of the skin, you should steam your face by pouring boiling water over lime flowers in a good wide baking bowl, putting your face in the bowl and covering your head with a towel as if you were taking the Friar's Balsam for a stopped-up head. Stay there until the perspiration runs from your face, keeping your eyes shut tight. But do not take this treatment more than once a week, and not more than three times in the month.

Conceiving a Child

To conceive a girl, give your crescent a good splash of vinegar, rub well in, then inject a pipette or two well up inside yourself. This will not ensure a female but lessens the odds of a boy by a good margin, acid being inimical to male sperm. To conceive a boy, carry out the same process, using milk instead of vinegar, alkaline being inimical to female.

Conceiving, Difficulty in

First of all you must ignore that worthless superstition that you have a greater chance of conceiving if you copulate in the fields, or close to a growing thing or an erect object such as a standing stone or a tree. In practical terms you have a smaller chance outdoors, as indoors the man will be firmer and may the more easily penetrate and plant his seed the deeper when two persons are at their ease in a good sensible bed, than when you are stretched out on the hard ground with little spring in it, and surrounded by cowpats and nettles, not to mention workers and wasps and folk out for their walks. Conception on a Sunday is impossible, and the fields are all very fine and romantic but they make for a crowded quilt.

The old folk used to say that some women who could not conceive got themselves pregnant by rubbing their bellies against the belly of an already pregnant woman. That is another piece of idle nonsense. If you wish to conceive, you had better rub your belly not against a woman but against a man. That is the only way to conceive – sparing the presence of the Holy Ghost – with sperm in your belly and not with these old wives' blethers in your brain.

Conception, To Avoid, An Old Remedy

If a man is like the tomcat or the bull, you should keep a stale fish beneath the bed on his side. Put it where he cannot discover it. For example, loosen a floorboard and plant the fish underneath. The bad smell will occupy him and will take his mind off intercourse more effectively than leaving off the washing of your private parts, which, besides being unhygienic and liable to start up an infection, can in some men work the other way. Napoleon would send word to Josephine three days before setting off for home from a campaign, that she was on no account to wash herself until he arrived, and then only afterwards.

Of the alternatives a headache is the feeblest excuse, though only a brute will say that it is not your head he is entering into. Instead plead constipation. *Inter urinas et faeces,* as St Augustine saw it, is that much closer to the crux than the head, and the very thought of it, like the bad fish, will put him off.

If in spite of your best efforts to avoid intercourse he has sown his seed in your fertile crescent, then to stop it waxing, do the following. Get to your feet at once. If you are by the sea, take a brisk walk down to the shore and give yourself a good salt wash. If it is winter, or the weather does not permit, use the pump or the tub, after throwing in two good handfuls of salt. Above all be upright and active on your two feet for up to an hour at least after intercourse. This gives the unwanted seed an uphill struggle, and many that you have not already bedraggled will be like Sisyphus and never arrive at the desired point.

Constipation

You need: ½ lb of figs, 1 oz of senna, 4 tablespoonfuls of Fowler's treacle. Chop the figs and mix all up. Take only a level teaspoonful at a time, and for a child only a touch on the tip of the spoon.

A good stick of rhubarb is another effective cleaner out of lazy or inactive bowels. It must be chopped and stewed. Only the desperate will use it as a gomph–stick.

Conversation

This is one of the fast vanishing arts of civilisation, as more books are printed that are less worth the reading, the telephone takes the soul out of talk, and public houses are dens of drunkards where you will not hear a single coherent sentence. The coffee houses are long gone. To cultivate this art you need like minds and kindred spirits, a good bill of fare, and a wise wine merchant; and you must also seek out wisdom with the owl, who hunts his supper at night. 'Day unto day uttereth speech, and night unto night sheweth knowledge.' That is the Psalmist's best piece of wisdom. You must be ready to stay up late to follow it, to begin your conversation with the owl and end it with the cock. Dr Johnson was the greatest practitioner of this art, and although his wit was constant, his habits were nocturnal. Conversation was his armour against melancholy, and his antidote to illness and death. The great Boswell illustrated this, and knew how to draw him out, which is another art of the great talker.

Copper Kettles, To Clean

Slice a lemon in half. Dip one of the halves in salt and rub the kettle well. If necessary, repeat the process with the other half. Run the kettle under clear, cold water and dry and polish up with a cloth.

Corned Beef Hash

He said well who said that an army marches upon its stomach. As for the Battle of Waterloo, it was not won on the playing fields of Eton, for it was not won at all, and indeed not by Wellington, but by treachery if anything. Subsequent battles have had little to do with Eton and more to do with bully beef, which, though plain fare to many an old soldier, provides the simplest yet most succulent of dishes if properly prepared.

To serve up corned beef hash, take cooked corned beef and potatoes either in equal amounts or mix with a preponderance of potatoes, which is to be preferred. Grate in plenty of onion, shred in a green pepper, and add pepper and salt. Heated until piping hot, this produces a most nourishing, savoury and filling dish, providing you have remembered to stir in a good few knobs of butter as the dish reaches its hottest before serving.

If you are not in the field you may make a delicacy out of this simple fare by spreading the steaming hot hash thickly onto slices of toast, done thinly and crisply but well buttered. Onto each well-spread slice slip a poached egg done just to a tee and no more, sprinkle with finely chopped parsley, pepper and salt, and serve as caviar to the general. For this even Bonaparte might have conceded an Anglican, or even an American victory, in the kitchen, if not in the field.

Coughs

Horehound is excellent for coughs, especially in the old and the asthmatical. Or use the root of the wake-robin, dried and reduced to a powder, and mixed with honey or in syrup. Dr Robinson's Receipts for coughs are as follows:

GENERAL COUGH

2 tablespoonfuls linseed, 4 oz liquorice root or Spanish juice, 4 oz elecampane root, 3 quarts water, boiled down to 3 pints. Dose: a wineglassful four or five times a day.

GENERAL COUGH, ANOTHER

1 drachm powder of tragacanth, 2 drachms syrup of white poppies, 40 drops laudanum, 4 oz water. Shake the powder in the water till it is dissolved, then add the others. Dose: a teaspoonful three times a day.

ASTHMATIC COUGH

2 good handfuls coltsfoot leaves, 1 oz garlic, 2 quarts water boiled down to 3 pints. Strain, and add 8 oz sugar, boil gently for 10 minutes. Dose: half a cupful occasionally.

CONSUMPTIVE COUGH

2 pennyworth each of sanctuary, horehound, barberry bark; 1 pennyworth each of agrimony, raspberry leaves, clevers and ground ivy; 4 oz extract of liquorice; ½ a teaspoonful of cayenne pepper. Gently simmer in 2 gallons of water for half an hour. Dose: half a cupful four times a day.

Courts

Courts for cowards were erected, churches built to please the priest; prisons are built with stones of law, and brothels with bricks of religion. Stay out of all four, and improve on Burns and Blake.

Cowslip Wine

The freckled cowslip is on the wane, which did so well for colds and freckles and wrinkles and spots; but still if you can get 5 quarts from a good old pasture or an unspoiled verge, then add: 1 gallon of water, 4 lbs of loaf sugar, 1 sweet orange and 1 lemon to the gallon; and you will have the makings of the most delicious of country wines.

Slice the oranges and lemons and put all into the barrels; pour water cold from the pump and a little yeast. Stir every day till it has done fermenting, then stop it down, and in seven weeks it is fit for use. Have a care that your barrel is larger than the quantity you make. At least a half bottle of brandy to the gallon is to be put in after it has done fermenting, and a whole bottle will make it hot as Satan's hoof and with a kick to match.

Creation

When you consider the heavens and the earth, and all that in them is, you should also consider this observation: that the possibility of the universe arising out of an accident, or occurring in some other arbitrary fashion, is akin to the likelihood of Dr Samuel Johnson's Dictionary having been formed as the result of an explosion in a printer's shop.

Credo, Creeds

You must form your own creed in order to live truly. Those which have been written were devised by others for others, and upon them Miss Emily Brontë pours rightful scorn:

> *Vain are the thousand creeds*
> *That move men's hearts; unutterably vain,*
> *Worthless as withered weeds*
> *Or idlest froth amid the boundless main.*

Be like her, who could give her own credo in five words: *No coward soul is mine.*

But be also like Invictus, who did not possess Miss Brontë's great belief, but was content, no, not content with his own, but notwithstanding held his own, unflinchingly, unafraid, bloody but unbowed, the master of his fate, the captain of his soul.

Cucumbers

They should always be cut at the thick end to start with. Frequently there is a bitterness at the thin end, which can mislead you into supposing that there is a bad quality to the whole cucumber. This is almost never the case. But be sure never to slice the cucumber until you are ready for it to come to table. Then the whole cucumber is perfectly digestible. Never eat an old cucumber that has lain sliced for any length of time; and if it is unfinished, then simply stand it up on end, with the cut end in a bowl of water.

Cypress

The cones or nuts will arrest a heavy menstrual flow and will put a stop to involuntary urination. They will likewise stop the bleeding of the gums and will help to fasten loose teeth in the head.

Daisy

The tops make a passing fair whisky and may be added to poultices for treating bruises. The old folk called them bachelor's buttons because young girls pull them and make chains to enslave the free.

Dandelion Wine

Gather a gallon of the bright yellow heads, no stalks, and do this on a bright May morning or a warm day in April, early, before the bees get busy. Put the heads into the largest jelly pan and pour over them double the amount of boiling water, fresh from the spring. Allow it to cool and to stand for two whole days, during which time it should remain covered, though from time to time you should give it a good stir.

After the two days are up, add to the mixture orange and lemon peel from two of each, very finely chopped, and let it bubble on the heat for half an hour, but not too fiercely; after which you should put all through the sieve into a basin containing 4 or 5 lbs of lump sugar. Pour into an old cask, not a new one, along with the oranges and lemons well pulped, and allow to cool, after which add sufficient yeast, no more than ½ pint, and follow the usual steps. When the fermentation is finished and all clear, put into well-washed, well-stoppered bottles. On Christmas Day at the earliest you may drink to a May memory, fields of yellow suns, and if you have kept it coolly cellared and rightly chilled, you will enjoy the most beautiful glass of Yuletide wine.

Dawn

Try to rise with Aurora, whatever the weather or season. This is an easy matter in winter, when the sun rises so late you will be up long before him in any case, but as the year wears on from spring into summer, you should accustom yourself to rising a little earlier each day. To be up before the sun puts you into an ideal frame of mind for dealing with the day's business, and the rest of the day will be that much easier when you have seen to things at an early stage. Nothing is more soothing and pleasurable than the quietness of the first dawn hour, which may be the only hour of the day which you may have all to yourself. The light is never the same following the sunrise. The painter Corot used to say that by 9 o'clock there was simply nothing left to see. Be like the painter and the poet, then, and see each dawn, whether it be left-handed, rosy-fingered, or come up like thunder, outer China 'crost the bay.

Days of Our Years

The days of our years are three score and ten; and if by reason of strength they be four-score years, yet is their strength labour and sorrow; for it is soon cut off, and we fly away. (Psalm 90)

If you have not died in the womb, or fallen prey to infant mortality, or to a young girl's greensickness, or to the dangers of childbirth, or if persistent pregnancies and perennial breeding have not worn you to a shadow, and you have not dwindled into a premature grave, then if war, sickness, accident or disease also keep their distance, your chances may be strong for a long life. You will in all probability outlive your husband, and some of your children. But as time goes on, your senses and memory will begin to fail, your brain will recede, your bones grow brittle, your sinews stiff and your sleep irregular. You will suffer from constipation, poor appetite, reduced affections, and the perennial ingratitude of friends and children. Your family will wait for you to die. That is when you may begin to wish, like Job, that you had been stillborn, and gone straight from the womb to the tomb.

Remember then thy Creator, in the days of thy youth, while the evil days come not, nor the years draw nigh when thou shalt say, I have no pleasure in them. (Ecclesiastes 12:1)

Of what use then is a long life? Do not hope for it. Vanity of vanities, all in vanity.

Days to Keep

New Year's Day. Before midnight on the previous day you must sweep out the dirt of the old year from all the house, and when the bells ring in the new, everything should be in spotless order. Do not go into a new year with a cobweb in a corner, but start as you mean to go on, and as you mean to finish.

Easter. Boil your bairns' eggs in good strong thick tea, till they have gone a good, golden brown. After that let them take them along to the braes and roll them on to the rocks to crack open. Ministers say it is the rolling away of the stone from Christ's tomb, but it is older than the church by a long chalk. An egg is a new life and a rolling circle a never-ending one, eternity. Your children will not care about that. But they will enjoy the eggs well enough.

May Day. Get up early on the first of May, before the day dawns, as you always should, and wash your face in the dew, if there be any, and if you reach it before the sun has got to it first.

The summer solstice. A good time for whin burning.

Halloween. There are no ghosts or ghouls out more than on any other night of the year, but the children like to think so. Encourage them in this fantasy, for they like to be frighted, and let them dress up in all the old clothes you can rake out from the bottom of the kist. The guising is a good thing for them and you should get them each a turnip lantern and send them out for their apples and nuts. When they come back in they can dook for them. And hang them up some treacle scones from the washing line.

Martinmas. The old folk used to start the slaughtering of the beasts dead on this day, and the 11th day of November is as good a time as any around this time of year to provide for the winter. And bless the poor pig, for its time has come.

Yuletide. Well before Christmas get a good thick birch clog for the fire, and strip it of its bark, so that when Christmas comes it be fine and dry. It should be big enough and solid enough to burn that night but to be taken out of the fire for the following Christmas, for you should always use the half of last year's brand to light the next log, keeping it in a dry place till that time comes round again.

Plenty evergreens for the mantelpiece, fir, spruce or pine, and the holly and ivy from the estate. Hang up the mistletoe above the door, for all that pass through to claim a kiss, for kissing is a kind thing at Christmas. And never mind what the old folks say about the mistletoe, that the pagans bowed the knee to it and that it was the forbidden tree in Eden, causing Adam's death, and Balder's too. Both died because of blindness and a woman, we are told, but the truth is that they died because of themselves, and the woman ends up with the blame, being easier to pick at than the mistletoe, which grows high.

Plough Monday, Monday after Twelfth Night.
The horses will be out again and you should give the beast half an apple and cast the other half into the start of the first dreel. But the men will have been ploughing the sea for ten days already.

Dead, The

The Bible says that 'the dead know not anything' but that was written by a man (the Preacher) who was not dead, and who himself knew nothing about the subject of which he spoke. If you seek the dead you need do nothing, for the dead are all around us; their atoms are in the air you breathe, and they come out as leaves and plants, as all flesh is grass, where the white hand of Moses on the bough puts out, and Jesus from the ground suspires.

Avoid at all costs those charlatans, mediums and spiritualists, who would lead you to the dead in their séances, for they are either ignorant, foolish, or malicious, preying upon the needs of the bereaved for greed or glory; and you can talk to your dead without sitting in the dark, or conversing with some Red Indian chief, whose happy hunting-ground slumbers you have supposedly disturbed. There are clairvoyants who are not charlatans. But let them alone, and if the dead wish to come to you, they will do so without the aid of mumbling fools and a pile of cheesecloth.

The dead are merely enjoying the quiet nonchalance of eternity before taking up their simple wardrobe and starting for the sun. They have met the postponeless creature, taken the cure for all diseases, the dressing that unbandages the soul.

The best words on the dead were written not by the Preacher but by the inimitable Miss Dickinson, who teaches you not to fear the dead. Hear her on those who dropped like flakes and persisted in the seamless grass. The thoughtful grave tucks them in from frost. Safe in their alabaster chambers sleep the meek members of the Resurrection, rafter of satin and roof of stone. No king of terrors here, but a thoughtful friend, one who reminds you that this quiet dust was gentlemen and ladies, and lads and girls, was laughter and ability and sighing, and frocks and curls.

Only Emily Brontë emulates the beauty of this thought in the last words of *Wuthering Heights*, surely the most beautiful sentence in English literature: '*I lingered round them, under that benign sky; watched the moths fluttering among the heath and hare-bells; listened to the soft wind breathing through the grass; and wondered how anyone could ever imagine unquiet slumbers for the sleepers in that quiet earth.*'

73

Dead Cheese, To Resurrect

Hard cheese, though it's as hard as Pharaoh's heart, can be saved. A cloth soaked in white wine should be wrung out and wrapped around the cheese for a few hours till it regains its texture. Vinegar will do as well as white wine.

Debts

You are asked to forgive your debtors. But if you have been neither a borrower nor a lender, then your compassion will not be put to the test, and nor will your creditors, for you will have none. Never owe a penny. And if penury pinches to the point of starvation, then beg; for true alms come from the heart, not from the purse, and charity is not credit.

Decanters, To Brighten

Insert some crushed eggshells, pour in half a pint of water, and shake as if you had Wallis Simpson by the neck. Then rinse, using cold water.

Or, pour in a heaped tablespoon of salt and a dessertspoon of vinegar, and shake it just the same, rinsing afterwards.

If it is an oil decanter or container and you wish to use it for another purpose, fill it with fine ashes, cold, from the fireplace, and put the bottle in cold water, which you bring slowly to the boil. After a while take away from the heat but allow the bottle time to grow cold in the water. After that make soap suds, wash and rinse in cold clear water, and the inside of your container will be once again bright and free from oil.

If the decanter stopper gets stuck, as they sometimes do, pour a little olive oil around it so that a few drops seep into the blocked mouth. Do this near the fire, then simply give the stopper a tiny tap to loosen it.

If two glasses are stuck one inside the other, simply run some warm water into the inside glass. Hot water leads to a quick divorce.

Diaries

Maintain a diary all your days. A diary is a doorway to a second life, running parallel to the one you live, and produces even a third life, for by recording the day's events, you preserve the days like berries. You may return to that day, taste it, and live it over again, but without that act of preservation the day has gone; it is nothing. More than this, by preserving your days, you will allow others to live that day for themselves, that hour, that afternoon, should they read your record, a day culled from the past, perhaps even hundreds of years from now; and this indeed is the aim and enjoyment of all writing, however humble, to seize the day, and to store it away on a secret shelf, out of reach of the Reaper and his swinging scythe.

Diarrhoea

To one quart of blackberry juice put one pound of white sugar, one tablespoonful of cloves, one of allspice, one of cinnamon, and one of nutmeg. Boil all together for a quarter of an hour; add a wineglass of whisky, brandy, or rum, depending on the taste of the sufferer, unless it be a child, in which case rum is to be preferred. Bottle while hot, cork tight and seal – this is a specific in diarrhoea, where corking and sealing is the desired effect. Give an adult a wineglassful and a child half that quantity, and the problem will be so quickly stopped that the patient may wish he had not been cured so speedily and will request another glass. But if the case is severe the dose can be taken three or four times a day until the condition is cured or the person concerned is happily imbibing the treatment.

Dogs

Greater-hearted than human beings, their legendary loyalty and affection deserve your respect, and there is no better representative of the dog's general qualities than Argos, Odysseus's faithful friend, who was the only one to recognise his master when he came home from his wanderings after twenty years. The dog had been vilely neglected in his master's absence, and lay weak and unloved and full of lice. But sensing Odysseus's return after all those years, he dropped his ears, wagged his tail – and died. He lacked the strength to come to his master, and his master could not come to him because of the danger of discovery. All he could do was to wipe away a secret tear. It is one of the truest moments in great literature, a man and a dog, and a bond between them that puts most human ties to shame.

Dreams

They come as the multitude of the day's business, but they may also come from God and from below the grave.

If you dream you have lost a tooth, it's a friend who will perish. A front tooth is a closest friend, the further to the back the less near and dear. If a rib is missing or is being torn from you, you will lose your spouse. You will not feel pain at the time but the pain will come later, when the thing itself happens.

To dream of a wedding is to dream of death. If you dream of the marriage of a particular person, whether that person be already married or not, he or she is doomed, and may already be dead or dying by the time you wake up. Never try to warn them of their fate, in any case. For what is before you will not go past you.

But if you dream merely that someone you know has died, this usually means nothing at all, and you may put it from your mind.

Dress

It has been said that a woman is better out of the world than out of the fashion. This is but one of the many observations of the ignorant on the matter of female dress, where the opposite is the case: that if you are a slave to fashion then you are a slave to the world and better quit of it, or it of you, for fashion by its very nature is a shifting and superficial thing, leading to idleness, ignorance, wastefulness and greed.

The best female dress is the dress that God gave you, and you should wear it unashamed and indeed with pride, and refrain from those hideous garments which do injury to the female body, and are as injurious to health as to the eye. *Enquire Within* gives good advice on this subject. Greek women walked freely and easily, unconstricted by bandages and ligatures and stays, and the loose and flowing robes in which the Grecian artists depicted them perfectly reveal the form and proportions which ought to be the delight and dignity of the modern woman.

Do not cut yourself in two like a wasp and not like a woman, but display your womanliness so that your shape accords as closely as possible with what lies beneath; the clothed woman corresponding to the naked woman as near as decency allows. If you have any doubts on this point they may be dispelled at a glance by observing those representations of the great Mother of Mankind, so marvellously executed by Monsieur Doré in his illustrations of Milton and the Bible. Time did not exist in Eden, and Eve is no hourglass there. Yet it is thirty years since she was thus portrayed so triumphantly as a model to modern woman, who, a generation later, continue to persist in distorting their glories and impairing their well-being. For any confinement of nature is not only bad taste but is inimical to health.

Dutch Lover

It has been said that even a Dutch Oven would not warm him up; and it is difficult to bring to mind any Dutch Don Giovanni. But then he is dependable, unlike the libertine, who was warmed by the ovens of eternity.

Earache

You need a good large onion, onion juice being one of the most efficacious among remedies for earache. Take a small length of good heavy brown wrapping paper and in it place a large Spanish onion. Wrap up firmly, give it a good wetting in cold water so that it soaks through, and roast this in the embers, but not in the flames of the fire. When the onion is soft, strip away the skin and extract the juice. You may do this by holding the onion in both hands over a bowl, or you may squeeze out the juice by twisting the peeled onion in a thin cloth such as an handkerchief. Bottle and stopper it and it will keep for a long time. As soon as the earache comes, pour a few drops into a teaspoon, warm the spoon till the juice itself is warm, but not hot, then drop slowly and carefully into the affected ear. This has never been known to fail to cure the earache, but be sure to plug the ear afterwards with a plug of cotton, also warmed, or dampened in the warm juice.

Early Death

This is upsetting in the least and grievous in the worst, but viewed reasonably, is not to be too much regretted. Remember that only the passing moment is your possession, and what has passed and is in the past, has instantly ceased to be yours, or anyone's; and so when you come to die, your loss is the same after seventy years of life as that of the person who has lived for seventy thousand years, or seven days, or seven minutes. The moment of death makes you equal with all others. However, the longer your life goes on, the greater must be the goodbye, and the accumulation of all that must be left behind. Regarded in this way, an early death may even be taken as an advantage; and, if Sophocles is correct, those whom the gods love die young.

Early Peas, To Keep Mice Off

Bring from the beach a pail of sea sand and strew your peas quite thickly with this. It annoys the mice by getting in their ears, and as they are fastidious creatures they will go elsewhere to eat their peas in peace and without the inconvenience of the sand. Imagine your own ears full of sand. You can wash them out in a minute, but for a mouse, whose ears are also more delicate than ours, it is less easy to rid himself of this irritant. Sea sand is better than builder's sand as it is grittier. This is an infallible remedy and does no harm either to the mice or the peas.

Early Rising

The Psalmist says that it is vain for you to rise up early, to sit up late, and to eat the bread of sorrows; but the Psalmist was not minding a house; and if you do not rise up early there may be no bread for you to eat at all, or for your hungry ones. Only by starting the day with an especially early breakfast will you find that time will be saved and the rest of the day go well.

Late risers are not late livers, and it is action, not sleep, that is good for the constitution and the blood. Moreover, it has been calculated that if you rise at 5 o'clock instead of 7 o'clock, then in the course of forty years you have gained almost 30,000 hours; which is the equivalent of eight hours a day for ten years; so that you will have added ten years to your life. Imagine spending those same ten years asleep; and if you further reflect that sleep is a sort of death, broken only by dreams (which by their nature do tend to be troublesome), then late risers are wasters of their own lives and are daily prefiguring their own deaths. Bathe in cold water the moment you rise, every morning without fail, and your life will not only be long but healthy too, and vigorous.

Eglantine

For alopecia, pound to a paste those spongy balls which are found upon the sweet-briar, mix with wood-ashes and honey, and apply to the scalp. The powder of the dried pulp, applied to your private parts, will stem the whites.

Elder

Burn the elder, rue the day,
One within will pass away.

Do not use it for firewood, it is one of the poorest, and the old charcoal burners refused to burn it for its dark connections. Nor would the old folk furnish a crib out of the elder wood, especially the rockers, for fear the infant would be rocked to death by the dark ones while you slept. The old folk would never burn it inside the house for fear of death and the devil.

Use nothing in your kitchen either that has been made with elder, or that has elder in it, not as much as a spurtle, if you want to avoid a scalding. The tree has been known to uproot itself and roam the country roads by night, hiding up lanes and killing folk stone dead in their chairs and beds by looking in at them through their windows, attracted only to those houses that contained elder somewhere within. Never put a lighted candle in a window where an elder grows outside nearby. These may be old superstitions, but why attract attention to yourself and put such things to the test, when there is no need? This was the tree, remember, on which Judas hanged himself, and so it is cursed. Yet it has a lovely fragrance and has been known to heal and protect besides terrify and betray. A fickle tree, it is famous among men for its two wonderful wines: the dark port wine from the berries, and the summer white from the flowers. When you pick the latter, however, you must do so in full sunlight and on a hot dry day.

Elm

Elmwood flames are slow and cold,
Elmwood burns like churchyard mould.

The old saying is a true one, except that when well-seasoned and all dried-out, elm burns pretty well, but not when it is wet. Yet elm is eternal underwater and is used for the piles of river bridges and for the keels of our ships. The inner bark you can eat when the tree is newly felled, and it is extremely effective in treating digestive disorders. Boil a handful of bark in a pint of water, strain, let cool, and drink morning and evening until the stomach settles.

Emancipation of Women

Although this has come far indeed, it is an absurd irony of existence that while you may help to choose the Prime Minister, you cannot choose your own husband but must wait for him to choose you. For months and years you await a proposal when you have a much better idea in your own heart and head of the sort of man you would wish to marry. You are in fact much wiser than men in matters of the heart, as most men do not think with their hearts, and certainly not with their heads, but in an entirely opposite direction; and the sad result of this situation is a great many slovenly, peevish and fretful wives, who are domestic disasters because they married their opportunities instead of their preferences. You have suffered too long from Mrs Grundy, in spite of Mr G. B. Shaw's cynical assertion that it is we women who actually do the wooing. The next step in feminine liberation ought to be the right, not the privilege, to choose the man with whom you will be spending the next thirty or forty years, till death do you part, or until the one kills the other.

Envy

Envy and Ire shorten life. This is not true of all deadly sins. Pride and Greed, for example, may be so great in a person that they will stubbornly persist in fulfilling their own narrow and selfish intent throughout a long career dedicated to self; whereas Covetousness and Wrath gnaw at the innards like poisonous minerals, and eat the spirit into extinction.

Evolution

Much impertinent nonsense has been uttered and written recently concerning this subject, and there has been great talk about the Origin of the Universe and the *Origin of Species*, as if the two were connected, and attempts made to drag Mr Darwin into the arena of atheism, to conduct the gladiatorial combat against God on behalf of those who are too weak to challenge God themselves. You should understand one thing: Mr Darwin does not attempt to establish a primal cause for human life, or indeed for any form of life, he merely describes a process, without explanation as to what began that process; and he does not attempt to explain because you would have to be dead to understand it: the concept is beyond human understanding.

We owe much to Darwin (as to other scientists) because his theory of the evolution of life on earth actually supports the Bible, and in particular the Book of Genesis. Mr Darwin is in fact the best supporter the Book of Genesis ever had, because it should be clear to you – unless you are an idiot – that Genesis is about geological epochs.

The Bible does not call them Cambrian or pre-Cambrian or Jurassic or Silurian or Devonian – such terms were not thought of; it calls them *days*, which is the simple language of the fairy story or the myth; and again, only the idiot reads such a story literally, whether that idiot be a religious zealot, or an atheist who wishes to destroy the orthodoxy of the zealot's belief. Avoid the company of both kinds of zealots: you will learn nothing from them except prejudice and simplicity.

Yet there are those, even ministers of the church, who will tell you that this six-day wonder, the creation of the Earth, was completed on the first day of October 4004 BC, and at nine o'clock in the morning precisely: a belief as idiotic as the view that the real age of the earth (millions of years) disproves the existence of God. Holders of either view, ministers of religion or professors of science, ought to be dismissed from their posts for the simplicity of their minds.

Exercise

This is natural to man, as to animals, as we see in children, and it is entirely unnatural to allow a life of sedentary habits to produce the lamentable consequences that render us vulnerable to illness and disease. Walking is within the power of all, except those who are lame or otherwise prevented, and this should be combined where possible with running, wrestling, fencing, dancing, riding and sailing, the sea-air being famed as a promoter of health, and sea-sickness a benefit worth enduring as it improves the action of stomach and bowels and removes undesirable matter. If exercise is not within a person's power you should assist him by rubbing him vigorously either with the flesh brush, or, if he desires it, and you think it desirable, with your hand. Even those confined to bed respond well to such exercise.

Keep active, even when you are ill, if possible, for there are vultures and jackals both within you and without, who take note when the lion lies down to die.

Faith

Faith is what moves atheists and evangelists, and pulls down the blinds on their little minds. It is no more the prerogative of the believer than the disbeliever, for the existence of God can neither be proved nor disproved: therefore if you say there is no God you have faith in the limitations of your own reason; and if you say there is a God you are not using every part of the brain that God gave you, for reason is divine, but moves you to argue against the Deity, there being nothing logical about God. The fiercer the debate, the stronger the faith that informs the conclusion on whichever side of the question.

Use your rational powers, but do not misuse them to condemn faith, for a life without any kind of faith would be the dullest life imaginable, faith being a leap of the imagination. But blind faith in anything, belief or disbelief, arises from a denial of part of your humanity. Be a whole person, then, and let faith and reason play their parts.

Fascism

You will hear it spoken as a filthy word but it is simply an extreme form of nationalism, and as in all affairs it is the extremity that is wrong, not the essence of the thing.

Feet

Never neglect your feet, for they are the foundation from which you view the earth. In the primitive times your feet were sacred, for hunting, running away, bringing news. 'How beautiful are the feet of those that bring the gospel of peace!' Think of Pheidippides and Marathon, the runner whose last words 'We conquer!' were carried for miles on invincible feet. In your own life you leave behind your footprints that show others the way, as Seth, Adam's third son, was shown the way back to Eden by the footprints of his father and mother.

Nine hundred years after the expulsion from Eden, Adam on his deathbed begged Seth to bring him a drop of the Oil of Mercy from the Garden, and Seth found the way by following footprints that were nearly a thousand years old. So terrible was the sin of his evicted parents that whatever they trod on was burned up, never to grow again, so a blistered trail blazed the way for Seth, and the footprints of sinners showed the path back to Paradise. To retrace your sins is to find salvation.

Feet, being sacred, should be kept not only clean but also elegant, for if you have a true lover he will worship you by first kissing your naked feet. The great Puccini was not alone in first making love to the toes of his mistress. There is a peculiar satisfaction about this procedure that inspires an aria!

As for those with cold feet, a hot water footbath for ten minutes, followed by a cold plunge. Dry off, and rub till tingling. Then on with the stockings, thick worsted, and especially if an old person has slow circulation, keep them on in bed.

For sweaty feet, put some ammonia in the water, wash well, and rub in some ammonia directly. A little ammonia in the water will also help weary and throbbing feet, but the water should be cold, and you should add a slight splash of bay rum.

Fenugreek

For a stoppage in the womb, make a decoction sufficient to fill a large basin or shallow bath, and sit in it as you can. Or you may insert a suppository made of the juice of the herb, and convey it to the neck of the matrix, where it will quickly soften the affliction.

Fire, To Light, With Last Night's Dinner

If you have served potatoes, keep the peelings, let them be dried in the oven, and you will find that they will serve their turn as kindling when lighting the next day's fire and will do as well as wood, or even better.

Fish, To Intoxicate and Catch

To catch fish without net, line or hand but by intoxication alone: make a paste of equal parts of ground *cocculus indicus*, cumin seeds, fenugreek seeds, rice flour, flour and water. Make into balls no more than the size of small peas, and toss in the water. Very soon the fish will rise to the surface, and will allow themselves to be taken, drugged, without guddling or struggle.

Flatulence

The fart is a fine old friend to man,
It gives the body ease,
It warms up the blankets
And chloroforms the fleas.

If, however, you wish to forego the company of this flea-killing bedfellow, so rudely extolled, freedom from wind is an easy matter: two pinches, one of aniseed and the other of cumin, in hot milk. A cup of this will quickly rid the sufferer of this dubious companion. Alternatively, the party should take toast in the morning utterly cremated. This burnt offering offends the god of wind. The fart abhors burnt toast.

Forget-Me-Not

The sigh that heaves the grasses
Whence thou wilt never rise
Is of the air that passes
And knows not if it sighs.

The diamond tears adorning
Thy low mound on the lea,
Those are the tears of morning,
That weeps, but not for thee.

93

Nature does not remember, according to Mr Housman's poem. We do not know what nature knows, or remembers; so do not presume that nature will mourn for you, or do your mourning for you; but never forget your dead. Forget them not: they are always with you.

Garlic

Grubs and slugs are kept off the garden by garlic, and the same with moles, unless you need mole powder. Otherwise, two cloves of garlic in a mole run, and you will never hear of him again.

Garlic is the most infallible remedy in the world against the vapours, and all nervous disorders, especially those to which women are subject. Garlic is gold to a woman.

Garlic dissolves stones and takes away the gravel if drunk in vinegar. If the juice is squeezed out and boiled in a syrup, it wonderfully preserves the lungs, kills off coughs, and worms in the stomach. It also provokes the courses and urine. It is a good preservative against the plague, cures spots and blemishes, and eases pain in the teeth and ears. It has a special quality to dispel the inconveniences coming by corrupt airs and mineral vapours, or by drinking unwholesome water or liquors. It is held good in the jaundice, cramp, convulsions, piles, and like diseases proceeding from cold.

But it has not its virtues without its vices, for in cholerick persons it will increase the choler and send up ill vapours to the brain; and in those that are troubled with melancholy it will attenuate the humours, and cause strange fancies and visions in the head.

If any worm or earwig has crept into the head while you sleep, stamp some garlic in a mortar, lay it in water to soak, wring it out in a clean cloth, and put a few drops of liquor in the ear. It will either kill the worm or work it out with the wax.

A garden without garlic is a long way from Eden. The Egyptian and Roman empires were partly founded on garlic, for the slaves who built the pyramids and the soldiers who conquered the world were given garlic in good quantities. It may be effective against the hardening of the arteries. If however you are pregnant, abstain from garlic until safely delivered. Otherwise eat abundantly.

Chew a clove of fresh garlic each morning, except during pregnancy; it opposes many infections. It promotes digestion, circulation, and the flow of your urine. It will keep colds and vampires at bay, the former being the more likely visitors. Take half a dozen heads marinated in a pint of brandy as a remedy for rheumatism and all the old bone-aches. It may be taken both inwardly and outwardly, and rubbed well into the ailing parts. If a party be troubled with asthma, give the party a number of bulbs boiled soft and then dried. Put an equal quantity of good vinegar to the water, add sugar, and make into a syrup; pour the syrup over the dried bulbs, place in a jar, and stopper close; take a bulb or two each morning, fasting. Of the syrup of garlic, made of 1 oz of the expressed juice to 1½ oz of lump sugar, give an occasional teaspoonful to children for their coughs.

Chew it raw each day and you will have few coughs and

colds, and fewer friends in the first days. In time, however, your body will learn to absorb the aroma, and after a while, no one will notice.

Genevieve's Venison

Should a deer come your way, keep the haunch for this dish, which cut does best of all. You need:

> *a jug of Normandy cider, or the very best of Somerset*
> *about a quarter the amount of white wine vinegar*
> *a bay leaf*
> *some carrots and onions sliced*
> *some crushed garlic*
> *parsley, rosemary and thyme, but no sage unless for*
> *Scarborough*

With the above you make your pot. Do your onions well seasoned in oil, otherwise your mixture needs no cooking, but stir very well and let the haunch sit in it for four or five days, turning twice a day. Then remove and coat with strips of fatty bacon, after which place in the oven, basting after a while with brandy mixed with the liquor and a splash of lemon juice. Add some Calvados, or scented Volnay, or sweet Genevieve's fancy. Little can go amiss with this royal gathering of flavours, and it requires no garnish except mashed potatoes, with a little of the gravy poured over.

Genitals

On show in Eden, presumably, but not in art, Monsieur Doré has omitted to illustrate the first reproductive organs. In his *Formation of Eve* a flower obstructs the view, and Adam is awarded a blanket to conceal God's surgery. But, as our earliest ancestors produced offspring by the process that became universal, we assume their ownership of prelapsarian genitals, and not that they grew them following the Fall (or indeed *in* the Fall, as a theologian has recently argued, before ending his days in an American asylum). Why else would they have felt ashamed of their nakedness and hidden themselves from God?

Shame has no place here. Male and female created He them and enjoined them to be fruitful and multiply. Mr and Mrs Blake read Milton naked together and John Donne commands his mistress to show herself to him as liberally as to a midwife. Show yourself to yourself as liberally, as God gave you genitals for procreation and for pleasure, as for pissing in a pot; and though childbirth may be a labour of love, conception is a blessing; and those words 'in sorrow shalt thou conceive' are not those of God to Eve but of some old Pharisee of old time.

Ghosts

If ghosts trouble a house you should know that it is the ghosts themselves that are troubled, and they need be no trouble to you or your family. The spirit may be unable to rest perhaps because there is something hidden, some cash stowed away beneath the floorboards or in the earth, perhaps a document of sorts, title deeds or a will. Brand suggests in his *Antiquities* that perhaps you or the surviving relatives may be troubled about some matter, and that it is your trouble which is troubling the ghost; in which circumstance you still have nothing to fear. It is your own trouble you must banish, not the troubled spirit.

A ghost is often but not always preceded by a noise of some sort, or is accompanied by a sound. If it appears in the house it will mostly be at night during the hours of sleep, and will either approach the foot of the bed or will manifest itself there. If it appears to you, you should ask it two simple questions: who are you and what is your business? And you should ask this in the name of the Father, the Son and the Holy Ghost. Certain ghosts however may materialise and disturb the household without deigning to offer any reason for doing so, even when asked formally. In which case they must be laid, the usual destination and the one least acceptable to the spirit being the Red Sea, a location to which ghosts have been known to beseech exorcists not to send them. For there, at the bottom of the Red Sea, lie the hardest hearts in history, of old Pharaoh and his followers, Ramesses, the Pharaoh of the Oppression, hearts so hard and spirits so obdurate than even the waters of the Red Sea could not stop them beating on, even in death, and disturbing the deep; and time itself could hardly allay their tyranny. Who indeed would wish to be laid among them? Not even a bad spirit would wish itself down there with them, companions in hell.

The best thought is that there are ghosts everywhere and that they will not have, nor need they, keep you from your sleep, for there are few who have not seen or heard or smelled a ghost in their lives, even if they might not have been aware of it at the time, and might even have gone to their graves and become ghosts themselves without once knowing what it was they scented, heard or saw.

God

The creator of the universe. Some tribes call him Jehovah, some Allah, and there are many others. Christians adopted Jehovah, a bad stepfather, and endeavoured to improve him, for he was by his own admission a jealous god and a mass murderer – including women and children and whole cities. Perhaps something of Christ's respect for his Father's stormy hobbies persists in his vocation to bring not peace on earth but a sword. But God is neither an Arab nor a Jew. He is not even a man. He is not even a he. God is a spiritual force, working though science, through nature, and through human nature, and if you can partake of that force you will become like him, immortal. Some men and women have come close to it, Jesus Christ closer than anyone. He happened to be a Jew. But you have the same latent spirit, and whoever you are you are a daughter of God, equal to any man.

God and the Origin of the Universe

This is the most important question which as a thinking being you are called upon to consider: what caused the origin of the universe and what shall you call the force which brought it into being?

As for a cause, either there was a time when 'space' was empty (which by definition space is) or the components of the universe were already there, and 'space' was not empty, things having already gone on without a beginning. The question is, can something exist without a beginning? And the answer is that something else has to exist in order to start it off, and what caused that other thing to exist? The fact that something started means there was an effect, and every effect must have a cause. So when did that cause begin, and what was the cause of the cause? There is no way out of this. Can you really imagine nothing, absolutely nothing, and then all of a sudden everything, without that first cause?

Shakespeare puts it in five simple words: 'Nothing will come of nothing'. So things must have existed from all time, without having had a beginning – and that is impossible, and contrary to our knowledge of the world and to our experience. If a space is empty and something either suddenly or gradually appears to fill up parts of that empty space, and you say that this had no cause, you are talking nonsense; it is impossible. Or you say that something has existed from the beginning of 'time', whatever that may be, without ever having had a beginning; which is equally impossible. You might as well argue that all experience is an illusion, and life a dream. It is more logical to accept a spiritual cause for scientific events, as no scientist has yet produced a satisfactory scientific cause for the existence or creation of life, and as for Mr Darwin, he was least interested in such imponderable matters but preferred to study what he could observe with his senses.

Gold, To Clean

As soon as you pee and it is still good and hot, dissolve in it a little sal ammoniac and boil your ring briefly therein. You will be surprised what wonders a pee will work for your wedding ring, or for any piece of gold that is wearing a dirty face.

Golfers

Never marry one. The golfer is extinct from his waist downwards and from his neck upwards, the main portion of him being concerned with placing his shot in the hole as fast as possible. Precision, not passion, characterises the golfer. A most uninteresting specimen, with a colossal lack of soul.

Goose Grease

Keep all the fat from the Christmas goose in a large jar, and when the children have colds, spread some of it on thick brown paper and tie in on underneath their clothes. This will keep them warm and fight the infection.

Gossip

Tell-tale tit
Your tongue shall be slit
And every dog throughout the land
Shall have a little bit.

Grape, The

God's greatest invention. The Creator is always inspired; but on the third day he excelled when he created the grape, so extolled by Omar in his *Rubaiyat*. See Mr Fitzgerald's translation, as fresh and popular now as it was half a century ago. You cannot do better than to read his verse, and let the grape be your Gospel.

> *Ah with the Grape my fading life provide,*
> *And wash my body whence the life has died*
> *And in a winding-sheet of vine-leaf wrapt*
> *So bury me by some sweet Garden-side.*

Great Love

If you can aspire to that of Ruth, expressed in her pledge, there is none greater.

> *Entreat me not to leave thee, or to return from following after thee: for whither thou goest, I will go; and where thou lodgest, I will lodge: thy people shall be my people, and thy God my God: where thou diest will I die, and there will I be buried: the Lord do so to me, and more also, if ought but death part thee and me.* (Ruth 1:16–17)

Greensick Girls

When Hirapigsa and nettle broths have
failed, a greensick girl should be given a
lusty young man. If he should chance to
impregnate her, a mother must weigh
the affair in the scales of morality: a
deflowered daughter, or a dead virgin
to lay beneath the sod. But sometimes
the greensickness is no greensickness at
all, but a stirring in the blood, and a
quiet call for love, which it may be fatal
to deny.

To Grow Dark But Comely

To achieve a good sunburnt complexion in two days. There
is a great rage for this among some young women today,
to become like Solomon's Shulamite, but there is no need
to go to Lebanon. Simply rub your face with the juice and
skin of dark grapes, and then anoint yourself with unrefined
virgin oil, in which shake a teaspoonful of iodine to a pint
of the oil. In two days you will look like Cleopatra or the
Queen of Sheba.

Hair, Falling

Nettles will soon put a stop to this. You need 2 oz of nettles to 2 pints of vinegar, warmed not boiled, and let this stand till cool. Use the small nettles, not the towering ones, and rub the strained liquid into your scalp each day. Or you may add nasturtiums or burdock roots or both to the nettles and marinade the lot in a bottle of rum. If the remedy is for a man it will put hairs on his chest if they are not already there. If it be for you, you will have fifteen such men on your chest soon enough, singing serenades. The rum, burdock lotion and the nasturtiums need marinading for up to ten days before you strain. So bide your time and your patience will be paid.

Hair, To Keep a Gloss On Your

Put a sprig of rosemary in a glass of warm rum, and infuse. Add the melted marrow from a bone, preferably beef. Rub the lotion into your scalp and let it drink the goodness of this for an hour or so. Afterwards shampoo. Add a little vinegar and lemon juice for an extra sheen. And whenever you can, wash and rinse your hair in rainwater. If you do not have a rain barrel then collect it in a clean pail, the fresher the better. This rinse comes free and it comes from heaven, so you will have angel hair. As for hair tonic, rosemary and chamomile are best.

Haly Hoo

Sometimes when a child is born it comes into the world wearing a haly hoo, which is a holy or lucky hood, a little membrane or caul, surrounding the head only, part of the membrane that covers the foetus in the womb. This is of great good omen to the child itself, and whoever obtains it will enjoy good fortune and avoid dangers. In particular, and Brand confirms this, it is an infallible preservative against drowning, and our fishermen will pay any sum in the world they can possibly raise to come into possession of such a caul, even up to fifty guineas. They were also sold by howdy-wives to advocates and the like, for the special purpose of imparting eloquence to them in their trade. Should you hear of one born like this, go hot-hoofed to that household and obtain it if you can, especially if there be a seaman under your roof, or if you or one of your family might be likely to be undertaking a long voyage.

Hana's Goulash

Use equal quantities of onion and steak. Chop the onion exceedingly small but not through the mills of God and as fast as you can. A slow-chopped onion loses goodness. Then cook in fat till nice and brown. Pile on the meat, add salt to taste, and no more than a pinch of sugar and caraway. Now cook till the fat goes, stir in flour and plenty paprika, and add carrots and turnip and stock. This is a great winter dish and a man will bellow for more till the cows come home. A nice, rough, red country wine will suit it well enough.

Happiness

This is best achieved if you aim to stay out of the history books and to keep your annals blank, as Lucy Ashton sings in 'The Bride of Lammermoor':

> *Look not thou on beauty's charming,*
> *Sit thou still when kings are arming,*
> *Taste not when the wine-cup glistens,*
> *Speak not when the people listens,*
> *Stop thine ear against the singer,*
> *From the red gold keep thy finger,*
> *Vacant heart, and hand and eye,*
> *Easy live and quiet die.*

Miss Austen thought the best recipe for it to be a large income. Better to read Scott, or rather Solon, who calls no man happy until he is dead. Until then you may at best be fortunate.

Hawthorn

The Whitethorn or the May will grow fast and live long in your garden, giving good shelter from the cold south-east winds; besides which it will attract many birds to its thorny tangles, which provide you with song, but once provided Christ with his crown of thorns. The old folk for that reason may have been loath to let hawthorn into the house. If they are heavy in May, the 'snowfall' predicts a good summer, and an abundance of haws in September foretells a fine fall. The haws will make a good wine, but do not strip them bare for the birds' sake; and do not bring down a hawthorn but wait for it to fall, and if you lose one through age or a gale, it will give you fine logs and good charcoal.

Hazel

This is good for logs and charcoal, and like the hawthorn will predict the seasons for you, for a crop of thin-shelled hazelnuts will mean a quick, light winter, but if the shells are thick and hard to crack, expect a hard one, with fierce frosts and endless snows, deep into April, and even May, depending on the thickness and hardness of the nut. Nature knows things unknown to you and is your best teacher. She is also better prepared than man, and can teach you prudence and provision. Place a little stack of the hazel twigs just inside the front door, or on the mantlepiece, and you will be shielded from fire and storm, and the lightning diverted from the house.

> *Fear no more the lightning flash*
> *Nor the all-dreaded thunder-stone.*

The bolts will not hit you or the flashes find you out, and there will be no need for you to shroud the mirrors. And eat well of the nuts, which impart wisdom, imagination, and the power of love.

Health

'Know thyself' is the first rule, as in all things, as it is pointless to read advice about how long or little to sleep and work and eat and exercise and so on, when each person is made differently. You must follow those patterns that suit you best and you should pay heed to such universal advice as is given on these matters: mainly, that it is good to rise early, eat regularly, partake of fruits and vegetables, drink much water, chew your food well, exercise daily, be active in the open air each day, even for a short time, and always allow fresh air into your rooms by keeping the windows open both top and bottom, even in winter.

Look after your feet, eyes and teeth; take cold baths each morning all the year round; drink a little red wine each evening; and in the early part of the day exercise your lungs by lusty singing and in the evening by recitation of verse.

Learning by rote is also good for the brain, and it is an excellent thing to have a dozen or so long poems committed to memory so that you may recite them loudly on your walks.

Henbane

Like the hemlock, this herb should not be taken inwardly, but you may boil the leaves in wine and bathe your breasts with it when they are sore or swollen, or bathe a man's testicles to relieve his swellings. Women in the old times were known to rub the fresh juice into their naked bodies and so enjoy the sensation of flying. This procedure has no medical purpose and should you try it for exhilaration's sake, leave the broom in the corner, or put it to its proper use, for there are far better ways to fly.

Heroes

They do not make good husbands but they do make excellent verses, so never marry a man with heroic aspirations. It is better to read about him afterwards, when he is famous, calm and dead. Heroes are immortal, husbands are needed here and now, but only for a few years; and the best sort of husband in not a hero but a wondrous necessary man.

Herrings in Fur Coats

Take three large herring or half a dozen smaller ones, and marinade them for two days in a dill marinade, consisting of vinegar and water, two parts to one, and lots of finely chopped dill which you have first bruised gently. The herring must be filleted and chopped finely.

Now you need to make your mayonnaise. Use 4 large egg yolks, a good splash of vinegar, a teaspoonful of made mustard, and beat, slowly pouring in oil and sprinkling with seasoning to taste. Beat until thick.

After this you need:

3 middle-sized potatoes, boiled and cooled
1 big beetroot, boiled and cooled
1 onion, raw
1 egg, cooked

All must be chopped exceedingly fine, and from now on it is all a matter of layering: the onion finely diced, herring, mayonnaise, carrot, mayonnaise, herring, mayonnaise, beetroot, herring, mayonnaise, egg (hard-boiled, grated), herring, mayonnaise. Thirteen layers in a big dish, and to go with it a good, dry, crisp white wine.

Hiccuping

Take a cold key from an outside keyhole and press it suddenly into the back, as if you were trying to stop a nosebleed. Or, tell them to blow up a paper bag a few times, hold their breath for as long as they can, or deliberately try to produce a hiccup. Or, drink a glass of water from the opposite side of the glass, or drink off in one go a glass in which an egg-spoon has been placed. Or, give them a fright by coming up behind them without warning, shouting loudly in their ears and slapping them hard on the back. Or, try half a teaspoon of vinegar with just a pinch of sugar dropped in. Hart's tongue is also excellent for this. If all else fails, tell them that each hiccup causes the heart to lose a drop of blood, because of the connecting nerve, or tell them that they've already hiccupped 76 times and that the 77th hiccup means certain death. The shock of this intelligence, or the shock of the 77th hiccup itself, will either kill them or make them stop. Either way the hiccuping will come to an end.

History

History is not what happened but what you are told has happened, irrespective of what is true.

Waterloo, for example, was pronounced as a great victory for Europe when it was in reality the greatest of European disasters. It was Waterloo that led ultimately to the Great War, and to the present war. These awful events would never have unfolded had Napoleon succeeded in commanding Europe; Bolshevism would never have been born; and Hitler would still have been painting houses.

Hot Water Bottle, An Alternative

The stone ones are best, but it is better to make small bags out of fine sacking or flannel, and to fill these up with very fine sand which you have cleaned and sifted and then dried very well in the stove. Sew them up closely and cover with linen cloth, also to be sewed. These bags may be quickly heated up in the stove or in the oven and if placed near the hands and feet of the sick, will succour them with heat far better and longer than hot water bottles, which lose their heat and are less manageable. The sandbag retains its heat for much longer and is more easily adapted to areas such as the small of the back, where it may be tucked in without discomfort to the patient.

Hot Water Bottle, To Prolong the Life of a

1. Never use boiling water when filling the bag, as the repeated action of water that is too hot will more speedily perish the India rubber.

2. Press out the steam carefully before replacing the stopper, which will lessen the pressure inside the bag.

3. Never fill the bag completely, which will again reduce the pressure.

4. When winter is over and the bag is not required, empty it of water but blow some air into it before stoppering it again. Without air, especially in hot weather, the sides of the bag will stick together, and when you come to fill the bottle on the first night of winter you may destroy it in pulling them apart. If this goes unnoticed on the inside of the bag there is a risk of scalding in addition to the end of the life of the bag.

NB The stone hot water bottles will go on forever but are not so comforting or adaptable as rubber, especially when covered with a flannel cloth or container.

Housemaid's Knee

A familiar aphrodisiac in certain households. As to the condition itself, use an ice pack, or a towel wrung out of ice-cold water. Paint with iodine when most painful.

Huntsmen

A barbarous breed of men – and women – who must not be confused with gentlemen and ladies, of which they are neither; for a true gentleman or lady does not kill a defenceless fellow creature for sport, which is mere bloodlust, but perceives a kinship with nature's creatures, closer than any social bond, and which will encourage a person of soul to comfort and protect them rather than pursue and slaughter, not for food but for amusement. But as the huntsman loudly proclaims the pleasure to be taken in his occupation, it is only fitting that he be encouraged to experience these joys from the perspective of the hunted.

Strip him, therefore, of his lendings; remove his murderous guns; deprive him of the cheer of his stirrup-cup and the braying of his horn; and set him naked in the field, to be pursued by packs of ravenous wolves. If he escapes with his life and has discovered an unexpected pleasure in being pursued to the point of exhaustion, and with the terrified expectation of having his throat torn out, then allow him to bedeck himself again in his jolly habiliments, set him on his horse with cup and gun in either hand and his beagles barking about him, and send him on his way after the hare.

Impotence

A good cure for it is housemaid's knee, as many's the housemaid has taught the old master. Otherwise obtain from the farmer the bull's pizzle, root and bulbs, when the bull is over with it. Use only this to make stock, and for each year of the bull's life, boil it down for an hour. You will need a good-sized pot, since an old bull's testicles could grace a bowling green or disgrace the round shot on a man-o'-war, and the pizzle itself measure up to a good sized poker. It must be chopped into good pot-size pieces. When you make the soup after the stock, which may be of any variety, be sure to grate in plenty of carrot, or any other sweet vegetable, as these parts of the bull are not savoury but very strong. After a week of this broth the enfeebled man will spring up and take the field with honour.

Income and Outgoings

Keep your Accounts most carefully, detailing the cost of every article under separate headings, e.g. food, clothing, furnishings, crockery, domestic repairs, and so on, that you may ascertain the exact nature of the annual expenditure; and if it exceeds the annual income then you will be in a position to decide where and when economies should be practised. One method is the allotment of a fixed weekly amount to housekeeping, so that if one week exceeds it, the next must pay for it. This is a system which allows expenditure to be kept in check by being under constant observation. Above all, do not amass your bills or cause tradespeople to wait for their money. The golden rule is that if you cannot afford it, you cannot have it, and the misery of Micawber will never darken your door.

Infidelity

It is the distinguishing characteristic of the male sex. Expect inconstancy – and either you will not be disappointed or you will be agreeably surprised.

Ink Stains

Lemon juice; afterwards rub well with yellow soap and rinse out with cold water; but this must be done at once.

If the ink is on mahogany, add half a teaspoonful of oil of vitriol to a tablespoonful of water. Dip a feather in this and touch the stain. But be eagle-eyed, for if left too long a white stain will appear and be immovable. It is best to rub quickly if not removed, and repeat.

If the ink is on the carpet, throw on salt repeatedly, then brush off. You may also blot up as much as you can, and pour on cold milk, again repeatedly, blotting or spooning it up, until little trace of ink appears in the milk; then cold water, and dry.

If the ink is on covers, wash out in strong running cold water; but if cotton, salts of lemon in hot water.

If on books, a solution of oxalic acid should be applied to the page. But an ink stain on a book, though ugly, is not inappropriate. Ink was the author's fifth original requirement, after idea, inspiration, paper, and pen. An ink stain need not cause undue offence.

Insomnia

Fill your pillows with hops. This will work well with some folk and not at all with others. Find out where you stand, or where the party stands. If you are a banker, take some exercise and fresh air; if you are a manual labourer, take some indoor rest; if you are tired but cannot sleep, take a bath and a glass of brandy before bed; if you are married, have intercourse; if you are not married, this is your choice. Intercourse works wonders for men, who will be snoring three seconds after, but not always for women. In the arms of the right man you will quickly fall into the arms of Morpheus. And it is so much better than counting sheep.

Otherwise, try onions. These are marvellous adversaries to insomnia and onions do not get you pregnant. Spanish onions are best, but any will do. Stew them, and eat a couple softened, or as a syrup, or as a soup, adding a little butter and lemon if you like, for the tender stomach. Do this before bed, but not before sexual congress. One course or the other is to be chosen, and onions and intercourse do not blend well. With such incompatible bedfellows, do without your onions, and let your man have his oats.

Intercourse, Overture to

For many men this consists merely in taking their trousers down. But a good opera should start with a great overture. And remember that you are not an instrument but a player too. Play together, and keep time, that is the important thing.

Intercourse During Menstruation

This is forbidden in the Bible, where it is referred to as your period of impurity. But this is nothing more than superstitious and primitive tribal law, of importance to the old Jews, but which need not concern you. There is nothing impure about menstrual blood: it is a monthly cleansing of the womanly system and a renewal of your procreative powers, a good token that all is in order, and a new broom to sweep clear your front room each month, as merry as the moon and welcome and pleasant as a new one. But if one or both of you should require intercourse during this period, take care to spread a large, thick towel over the sheet you lie on. Steep it afterwards before washing and keep it for this purpose only.

If neither wishes intercourse but one or both of you should require release, be guided by your inclinations, and do whatever nature prompts you to do; it will not be wrong. As for buggery during menstruation, or at any time, though nothing is sinful between man and wife, which is one flesh, and both consenting, buggery may be harmful and unhygienic, and should not be entered into lightly, if at all. Do you see animals buggering one another? The answer to that rhetorical is that God gave us a faculty not given to beasts: imagination. There are times when imagination needs to play. A wife can never be a whore with her husband, except in play, and sometimes it is good to play the whore.

Iron, To Keep Smooth

Clean your iron using candle-ends in a dusting cloth. If you do this shortly before doing your ironing you will find the action of the iron very smooth indeed.

Jasmine

Eat it before you sleep, and you will sing with Isaiah, 'Watchman, watchman, what of the night?' Or sew some of it into a little muslin bag and sew this into your pillow, to make your dreams prophetic. You will have visions as clear as day.

Jealousy, To Cure a Man's After the Birth of a Child

Jealousy is not uncommon in a man after childbirth, usually after the first, and especially after the birth of a male child. To cure this jealousy, which is a reaction of nature and not to be feared, you should let your man suck your breasts and enjoy a small portion of your milk, but not so much as will short-change the infant; and the infant alone should have the breast for the first three days. After that you may encourage your man to suckle you. There need be no limitation set on this, if it pleases you both. A sucked breast may never run dry, and a man fed on his wife's milk will never leave her.

Kissing After Garlic

Put a sprig of parsley into your mouth and this will banish the garlic to far off Transylvania, while you have your enjoyment. If you are not amenable to intercourse, or if you must prevent a pregnancy and your crescent is fertile, chew a clove or two of fresh raw garlic before retiring. This will keep the most ardent of men to his side of the bed, and will also keep out the figments of Mr Stoker's imagination, whose kisses draw blood.

Knicker Elastic

A good pair should keep a twelvemonth and if not washed over roughly should outlast the moon. In time, however, the elastic will grow dozent and must be renewed, unless you wish to conceive. Good, strong knickers underneath your nightgown will inhibit access to the fertile crescent. In this case also keep the chamber very cold, which subdues the temptation to get unclothed.

Ladies' Mantle

It is an aptly named plant: for when your flow is profuse and prolonged, this will cast a mantle over the Red Sea. Some women apply the leaves to their enlarged breasts in order to reduce them and return them to what they deem their proper form; but if you have healthy breasts you should be thankful for them without fruitless speculation on their proper shape and size, for there is no such thing, nature delights in variety and eccentricity, and it would be a dull world indeed both for men and women if all females sported the same breasts, or the same noses, eyes and ears. Other women, wishing to reduce the dimensions of their genitals, have bathed them in an infusion of the green leaves, whose astringent qualities have the power to contract and draw together the private parts; this is an effect welcomed by women wishing to appear to possess the characteristics of virgins, and deceive men by a narrowness and constrictiveness that is not their characteristic at all, but the effect of the herb. You may bathe yourself with perfect innocence in the green leaves if you have suffered an inward infection (the properties of the lady's mantle being well disposed to the healing of vaginal inflammation) but if you do so with a view to proposing a virginity that you no longer possess, that is another matter; and you need have little doubt that it will easily fool a man, as even wise men were willing to believe that a Lady of Rome, formerly of Nazareth, conceived as a virgin, aided not by a herb but by the Holy Ghost, and this is the lady from whom the herb derives its name.

Ladies' Smock

This is the lovely spring cuckooflower which provokes urine and is indispensable in the greensickness. Always have it ready for a pale virgin who shows no appetite; it grows between some young girls and the grave.

Leeks on Toast

Young leeks do best, with the rougher outer leaves trimmed away. Cut in lengths to suit, bring to the boil in water already salted, cook for twenty minutes, drain, place a knob of butter on top, and serve with a whiff of white pepper.

Lemon, To Prolong the Life of a

A lemon will keep a long time in water and may be preserved in a jar, though the water should be changed each morning.

Lemons

Your household should never be without lemons, they fulfil so many purposes throughout the house, quite apart from their everyday usefulness in Receipts, where they are a necessity. Lemon juice will serve as a cleaning ingredient; it will provide relief from painful bunions or corns; it is excellent as a hot drink for colds, especially at bedtime; it relieves bad headaches if a slice be rubbed on forehead, temples, and on the scalp, where it will also prevent or curb the loss of hair in both men and women, if rubbed in vigorously. It will also take the pain out of a bee sting or the bites of other insects.

Life

If this depresses you, remember it is a cause of depression which a good many must put up with. It may be a dream, a farce, a fitful fever, a poor play or player, a shadow, a stained glass window, a chequerboard of nights and days, etc., etc. The poets have found many images and expressions for it. Only one thing is certain: it is not a rehearsal. You will go on afterwards, but not in your present form, and this life you are leading is the only one of its kind you will ever have. It will not come again. Waste not, therefore, so that you will want not when the affair is over. The best life lived is the one that allows you to say with all sincerity at the end of it: 'I warmed both hands before the fire of life: it sinks, and I am ready to depart.'

Lifebuoy

This soap is a powerful disinfectant and exterminator of the various germs and microbes of disease. It is excellent for children and has cured in them cases of ringworm and eczema. Many grateful mothers have spoken of its beneficial effects. It is of course an equally excellent soap for ladies, rescuing you from contagion and disease, and cleansing, purifying and sweetening the whole house.

Lightning

If you are abroad during a storm avoid all trees, but especially oaks. If you are indoors, where you ought to be, it is a mistake to try to shut it out, for lightning, if hindered, will find an entrance where you may least wish it. You should therefore keep your windows open a little, and even the door ajar, to allow it passage. Some of the older folk shroud their mirrors, lest from the looking glass the lightning reflects back on them. This is unscientific nonsense, but hold no metal in your hand during a thunderstorm, not even the tiniest needle. Though you were inside a haystack, the lightning would find you out and put an end to your sewing.

Lisbett's Chowder

The best chapter in Mr Herman Melville's great epic is the chapter on chowder. All Nantucket seems to be imbued with it: clam chowder, cod chowder, there was no other dish at the Try Pots Inn, where the hostess wore a polished necklace of codfish vertebrae, the account books were bound in shark-skin, clam shells not cobbles paved the courtyard, fish-bones, not your own, appeared to be poking through your clothes; when you strolled along the sands you went slip-shod on cods' heads, and even the milk tasted of fish, with the brindled cow feeding on fish remnants. This fairly whets the appetite for the dish itself, emerging steamily from the kitchen: a smoking chowder, made of small juicy clams no bigger than hazelnuts, done with salted pork flaked in, mixed up with pounded ship's biscuits, and the whole savoury thing enriched with butter and abundantly seasoned with pepper and salt.

If that does not have you putting to sea, or making a beeline for the fish counter, you have no spirit for literature and you will never transmigrate into a fish in the next life. To try Betsy's chowder is to enter into the soul of the fish.

Any fish will do, but the cod is your man, and sovereign of the sea for chowder. Gently cook the cod or clams, or both together, in a little water, and remove them. Drop cubes of onion and potato into the stock, and cook until tender. The cubes should be pretty small. Now add the clams, or the fish, boned and flaked, and sufficient milk to make the soup. Once the milk is in you must refrain from boiling if you want a good flavour. Make a good quantity, as you will find the flavour even better the second day. Serve with salt and plenty of black pepper and Captain's biscuits. Or do it the Nantucket way for Hosea Hussey's sake, and mix ship's biscuits well pounded with the chowder. You will find it a good aphrodisiac for a man, and for a whole week he will want nothing but you and his chowder.

Loneliness

The rainy Pleiads wester,
Orion plunges prone,
The stroke of midnight ceases
And I lie down alone.

Long Life

You are advised to eat, sleep and occupy yourself well; to refrain from surfeits of strong drink; to avoid smoking tobacco; and to keep a healthy mind in a healthy body. You are advised in the Fifth Commandment to honour thy father and thy mother, that thy days may be long in the land which the Lord thy God hath given thee.

And yet how many sloths and gluttons and drunkards do you see who do no work, take no exercise, have no minds at all, and are the despair of their dishonoured parents? They go on to live long lives, outlasting those who have kept the faith and followed the rules and yet fallen foul of disease and death.

Live as you please, then, and instead of long life, aim to grow wiser and happier, both together.

Mad Dogbite

Wash the bitten part well, first with strong, hard, clear-running spring water, if you can; then wash again with a strong decoction of tobacco, and bind the wound with wetted tobacco, leaf or cut, but the leaf if it may be obtained.

Or, you may dissolve a pound of salt in a quart of water; squeeze, bathe; wash the wound with this liquid for one or two hours; then bind some salt upon it for ten or twelve hours.

Marriage

Marriage is legalised intercourse, but many are married in the legal sense who are not morally married at all. There is natural marriage and there is marriage devised by man, and your natural love needs no certificate to sanctify your relations with the man you love.

As soon as the ring is placed on your fourth finger you should keep it there for life and never change fingers for a moment, not even in fun, nor for comfort of any kind. The old folk used to think that there was a small artery ran from this fourth finger right to the heart. Doctors now say that was just superstition and that there's no such vein. Who knows what God hid in the body?

Marriage has many pains, but celibacy has few pleasures.

If you wish to reduce the pains, the golden rules are: never marry a teetotaller, or a man who does not smoke. And never marry an artist, for he will let you starve, your children go barefoot, and even his mother break her back for him at seventy years old, sooner than work at anything but his art, or earn a penny to keep you from the streets. He will fill the house with his genius, and you won't have a pot to piss in. And if you do, he will quickly paint you on it, and sell it from under your arse.

Marry in Haste

Repent at leisure. Adam and Eve offer the best example of that wise saying, and the advice is good. According to the old Jewish scholars Adam spent a mere twelve hours in Paradise – half a day, the timetable of events running as follows:

> 1st hour: God gathered the dust and animated it.
> 2nd and 3rd hours: Adam stood up, looked around, and became monarch of all he surveyed.
> 4th and 5th hours: he gave names to all the animals.
> 6th hour: that tired him out and God made him sleep while he opened him up and removed the rib out of which Eve was created. This is the first recorded use of anaesthesia by hypnosis.
> 7th, 8th & 9th hours: he married Eve and experienced up to three hours of married bliss – without intercourse. Most

bridegrooms do have to wait a few hours after the ceremony.

10ᵗʰ & 11ᵗʰ hours: he fell. So his marriage lasted only three hours before things began to go badly wrong, quite possibly the shortest example in history of conjugal bliss, and it took only two hours for the entire future of the human race to be blighted.

12ᵗʰ hour: he was thrust from Paradise along with his wife, the first recorded example of eviction.

Thus in half a day we have: the quickest birth, the shortest courtship, the worst marriage, the first eviction and the complete downfall of the species, and all before dinner. After that Adam took up gardening, thinking he was retired. But God told him the work was only just beginning. So we have the first employment. The Talmudists are silent on how the guilty pair spent their next twelve hours in bed, but if we are to judge from the arrival of Cain they wasted little time. They were guilty in any case and life was shorter then, in spite of the Hebrew system of years. Cain then killed his brother, the first murder, but where he found a wife from is another mystery. The one clear message is that hasty marriages are not a good idea. Other truths follow. To err is human, vengeance is divine, and you many repent for the remainder of your life.

Medlar

This tree has attracted the bawdy eye of poets, as to meddle with a maid invites a pun on its fruit, leading to much coarse talk, for example, from the mad Mercutio on the subject of open-arsed females and poperin pears (see *Romeo and Juliet* Act 2); and yet the fruit is reputed to cure unnatural longings in females, for buggery unquestionably, this being the doctrine of opposites, and like leading to unlike.

A strong decoction of unripe medlars arrests diarrhoea, and both leaves and fruits will stem the menses when the flow is profuse. The fruit, if dried just before rottenness, made into a poultice and applied to the kidneys, will also prevent a miscarriage. You may gargle with a decoction of the fruit; or a party may sit in a bath of these for the bleeding piles.

Melancholy

There's not a joy the world can give like that it takes away. Byron tells you all you need to know. Melancholy is the lot of man, and especially of woman, whose lot is to sweeten a sad world, but no thinking person of either sex can be glad.

The best cure for melancholy is a little wine and much reading, especially Dr Johnson and his *Rasselas*. This is a most consoling book, which, since it teaches you that happiness is impossible, persuades you to refrain from seeking it, and so allows you a kind of melancholic contentment.

To drive away melancholy, especially in February and November, put the stalks and leaves of burnet in a cup of wine, especially claret. Or take viper's bugloss, which is a great quickener of the spirit, also dodder, germander and the archangels. But beyond compare is a decoction of the thistle, which will cure you, as it will all those troubled by strange melancholies that seem to have no cause.

Men

Primitive beings in whose sexual organs sperm is forever building up, leaving them with a persistent need for intercourse; that is to say not intercourse with a particular woman but intercourse *per se*, often leading to affairs and follies.

Men endure pain less well than women and are in constant need of mothering. Many are tireless workers and incorrigible drinkers. Women may write as well but are let down by Bloomsbury snobs and such like, and in comparison with men they make poor painters and musicians. Yet without women men are as useless as castrated horses and tonsured monks.

Menstruation

As for the nonsense that has been talked or whispered or scolded on the subject, most of it is well worth your ignoring: e.g. a menstruating woman should not enter a field of cows for fear of curdling their milk, or a dairy for the same reason. If this were true, dairymaids would be unable to fulfil their duties for one week in each month, and would be in splendid isolation for three months in the year. As for the injunction not to swim during your period, as if by so doing you would turn the green sea red, and all the multitudinous seas incarnadine, the exact opposite is the case. The sea is astringent as well as infinite, and if you experience profuse or prolonged menstruation, there is, on the contrary, all the more reason to go sea bathing.

Mirrors

Pay no heed to that old custom of covering up mirrors during thunderstorms, for this is a country superstition, and lightning cannot leap back at you out of the looking glass. But take care not to break a glass. Breaking a mirror brings you seven years bad luck. Apart from this, mirrors should be treated with caution, as they contain not the truth but mere tricks of sight, not reality but illusion. If you look into the mirror and see standing behind you the image of one whom you know to be dead, never turn around, but walk backwards till you pass through the apparent substance of the image, and it will disappear. As for infants, they should be kept well away from mirrors until after they have cut their first teeth.

Monarchy

Hereditary monarchy is an absurd idea. Governments exist by stealing from the people, none more so than those headed by hereditary monarchs. They do not own you, though they would wish you to believe that they do; and their chief ally is the church, that preaches subservience when it ought to preach equality, the doctrine of the Bible.

Moon, The

Kill the pig when the moon is waxing and the bacon will be the better in the boiling; shear the sheep at the increase, but fell timber from the full to the change; all grafting operations are advised to be executed in March at the moon's increase when she is in either Taurus or Capricorn; have your hair cut when she is either in Leo or Aries, so that it will either stare like the lion's shag or curl like the ram's horn. If you want more of something, avail yourself of the moon's increase: if less, select the period of her wane.

Mortality

Let the knowledge of your own mortality never leave you, but never leave you afraid. Rather let it make you a better person all your days. For illumination on this subject you can do no better than look to the old poets, though no one befriended Death like Miss Dickinson, and with the exception of her verses, only Tennyson among living poets remains to repay reading, Mr Arnold being now acquainted with Immortality.

Mourning

When I am dead, my dearest,
Sing no sad songs for me;
Plant thou no roses at my head,
Nor shady cypress tree:

Be the green grass above me
With showers and dewdrops wet;
And if thou wilt, remember,
And if thou wilt, forget.

This is excellent advice from Christina Rossetti, as you mourn for yourself and not for the dead, who need no tears.

To drop a tear within the box
Where youth and years have flown –
Prophetic mourner, close the lid –
The coffin is your own.

The best thing is not to mourn but to remember, as Mary Coleridge does:

Some hang over the tombs,
Some weep in empty rooms,
I, when the iris blooms,
Remember.

I, when the cyclamen
Opens her buds again,
Rejoice a moment, then,
Remember.

Moving House

When moving house do not let the last fire go out. Build it up until you have a good blaze going, then shovel the flaming coals into a good strong bucket, free from holes or leaks. Two should carry it between them on a pole. Or, if the new house is not too far off, you may use the embers and transport the bucket yourself, wearing a glove or using a crowbar. Any method will do, so long as the fire of the old house lights the new, and the hearth flame never dies.

Music

Trust no man who is not truly moved by it. He will never truly love you.

The man that hath no music in himself,
Nor is not moved with concord of sweet sounds,
Is fit for treasons, stratagems, and spoils;
The motions of his spirit are dull as night,
And his affections dark as Erebus:
Let no such man be trusted.

(The Merchant of Venice)

Nails

A little lemon juice works wonders for the nails that are breaking and flaking. The best way is to rub them with half a lemon when washing, or, to a large wine glass of olive oil, add a splash of vinegar and a touch of boric acid. Stir well and dabble your nails in the mixture for half of an hour each bedtime. Also apply this treatment to your toenails, all the more so if you do not sleep alone. A sharp or ragged toenail is an instrument of torture in bed and can puncture many a promising bubble of pleasure. If an infection has occurred, and the skin around toenail or fingernail is red and sore, scald it as hot as can be borne with the water in which the potatoes have been boiled up for dinner.

Nakedness

Your nakedness is the work of God the Creator. Let men admire it – and grow religious between your sheets.

Nettle Stings

For this use nettle juice. Rub the stung part with the juice of the plant itself: a nice example of the old trick of fighting fire with fire. And remember the old saying:

Tender handed grasp a nettle
And it stings you for your pains.
Grasp it like a man of mettle,
Soft as silk its sting remains.

Nipples

There are various ointments for sore nipples but the best remedy is the white of an egg well beaten into brandy and applied frequently. Allow to dry naturally, and not with a cloth, but after drying use a nipple shield.

If your nipples are cracked during breastfeeding, apply this treatment at least one hour before the next feed, but wash off the eggnog before feeding. If the baby be a boy, he will soon enough gain a taste for nipples in brandy without encouragement in infancy.

Nose

God gave you this in his wisdom not merely for the purpose of scent, but in order that you may turn it up and look down on all those who think themselves your superior. All the better if you are the possessor of a good, long, straight nose; your look will be all the longer and the more commanding. It does not matter in the least if you are five feet tall, or how small your stature; your nose will ensure you rise above your 'betters'. When you enter a room, lift it in the air and use it like a blade. This will at once establish your pre-eminence among the 'better' class of folk; and once this matter is settled you may use your nose for its other purposes. If it is blocked, use eucalyptus leaves crushed; make an infusion and sniff well.

Old Age

When you are old and grey and full of sleep,
And nodding by the fire, take down this book,
And slowly read, and dream of the soft look
Your eyes had once, and of their shadows deep;

How many loved your moments of glad grace,
And loved your beauty with love false or true,
But one man loved the pilgrim soul in you,
And loved the sorrows of your changing face;

And bending down beside the glowing bars,
Murmur, a little sadly, how Love fled
And paced upon the mountains overhead
And hid his face amid a crowd of stars.

(W. B. Yeats, 1893)

Old Writing, To Revive

Have a pee, and in it boil up some gall nuts for several minutes. Let it cool, then take a good sponge, soak it well in the mixture, squeeze out, and gently rub the writing. You will find that the words shine out like bright black ink again, even though they have been fading fast these fifty or a hundred years.

143

Omens and Superstitions

* A dog howling in the night is a sign of a death in the family, or in the neighbourhood.
* A cricket behind the hearth is a good omen.
* The deathwatch beetle is a bad omen. .
* A robin will cover a corpse's face with moss, if it be the corpse of a rational creature:

> *Covering with moss the dead's unclosed eye,*
> *The little redbreast teacheth charitie.*

* The wren is noted also for this service to mankind:

> *Call for the robin redbreast and the wren*
> *Since o'er shady groves they hover*
> *And with leaves and flowers do cover*
> *The friendless bodies of unburied men.*

* Never kill a redbreast or a wren. If you do, you will break a bone before the year is out, and it may be a backbone or a neckbone, which will put you to your grave, and all for such a silly kill.
* A blue light coming from the fire or the candle flame signifies the presence of a spirit in the house, but may be nothing more than a sign of stormy weather to come.
* If the flame wavers, expect windy weather.
* If the candle is reluctant to light, expect wet weather.
* If the tallow builds up against the wick of a candle, it is

styled to be a winding-sheet and is therefore deemed an omen of death, and rightly too.

★ A flake of soot hanging on the bars of the grate signifies a stranger.
★ Sparkling means rain.
★ Soot falling means rain.
★ Fierce burning means frost.
★ If the down flies off the coltsfoot, thistles or dandelions, even in the absence of wind, it is a sure sign of rain.

Onions

Some think that old Pharaoh's lot must have got the sun and the sand into their brains when they worshipped onions. A cat is comprehensible, but imagine the humble onion as an object of deification. It was in derision of this notion that Diodorus Siculus wrote the couplet:

Such savoury deities must needs be good
That serve at once for worship and for food.

Onions, however, attack many infections and in the old days assailed the plague sores and the swellings in the armpits where the buboes appeared. An onion in the armpit, boiled, draws out poison, is good for the tubes, and is an excellent cure for insomnia and piles.

But onions should not be left lying unattended in the kitchen once they have been peeled, as they absorb any odours or infections which may prevail. This is precisely why they are useful against infections, and if eaten after being left awhile, may turn against the uninfected. Your onion is like fire, a good servant but a bad master.

Your onion also acts like garlic but it is milder: it promotes appetite, attacks insomnia and eases the bowels. Onions are good against old hard coughs and stubborn phlegm; they fight infection, kill worms, cure ulcers, heal burns, purge the head, improve the skin, counter lethargy, and burst boils.

Directions: for the boils, slice the onion in half and apply; for the worms, let the children drink the water in which the onions have lain steeped all night; for an inveterate cough the onion should be roasted and eaten whole with honey; for the head, the fresh juice should be snuffed up the nostrils; for infection, eat the onion with bread and salt; for burns, apply the fresh juice; for the skin, rub it with the juice mingled with vinegar; for sores and onions, make the onion hollow, fill it with treacle, then roast and beat well together; for general disease, cut the onion in two and tuck each half under either armpit naked, holding it there lying down, as long as possible. They did this in time of plague and in certain cases the onion drew out the poison.

Our Lady's Thistle

This is *Carduus Mariae*, better known by the country folk as ladies' thistle or milk thistle, and you should take it, but in small doses, when there is little milk in your breasts and you need to increase your supply. You will easily find it in June or July growing in the ditches and along the roadsides, and it also takes its name from the Lady of Rome, whose intercourse with the Holy Ghost put a child in her womb and milk in her breasts. Use the root and the seeds; but if you gather it in spring and boil the young plant without the prickles, it will cleanse your blood, changing it as the season changes. It should be added, however, that an infusion makes you pee, and must have made Mary make holy water.

Patriotism

Be sure to wave a large flag, as you do not know whom it will cover, or how many. And remember this simple verse:

> *Here dead lie we because we did not choose*
> *To live and shame the land from which we sprung.*
> *Life, to be sure, is nothing much to lose;*
> *But young men think it is, and we were young.*

Piano, To Care for a

Try to keep the temperature even in the room where it is kept. This is less easy in winter, but dampness and cold are much worse than excessive heat. Better too hot than too cold.

Dust is the next enemy after damp, and be sure to keep the lid closed and locked when the piano is not being played.

All other foreign objects should be kept well away. It is all too easy for pins and needles to fall between the keys, or breadcrumbs or tiny crumbs of food. The latter should not be brought within the vicinity of the piano.

Do not place an upright piano too close to the wall. A little distance will give a better sound, as will a clear top. Heavy piles of sheet music will deaden the tone. Polish frequently, including the keys, with a soft cloth dampened with a mixture of vinegar, lemon juice and water.

Piles, To Cure

Take a tin of Stockholm tar (not Archangel) and heat it in a pan of water with the lid off, as if you were heating a tin of kaolin for colds or boils. Any farmer or fisherman will give you Stockholm, or the blacksmith if he is shoeing the horses and sealing up the splits in their hoofs. But be sure to dilute it by a quarter with hot water, to prevent it from sealing, otherwise the sufferer will have a backend that will not let in the cold and wet, but will not let anything out either. Rub the diluted tar well into the afflicted area.

Or, take three leeks of different sizes but all large. Boil the smallest on the first day and eat all of it. Do the same on the second day with the middle-size leek, eating all as fast as you can. If on the third day the condition has not eased, boil the leek whole till it is howling hot, and use it like a Welsh lancer. The sufferer will need to grit his teeth for this, but worse things went on at Rorke's Drift and even iron men get piles, but only men of Harlech may stand the leek whole.

A handful of boiled buttercup leaves or freshly dug onions, steamed, with a large slap of hot vinegar may also be stuffed up.

Poetry

A life without poetry is like Omar without wine, and poetry is the wine of life. All poetry is sad, for poetry is the most private expression of our deepest longings, which can never be fulfilled, as man is born to trouble and discontent, as the sparks fly upwards, Shelley puts it best:

> *We look before and after*
> *And pine for what is not:*
> *Our sincerest laughter*
> *With some pain is fraught;*
> *Our sweetest songs are those that tell of saddest thought.*

Potatoes

The emperors of vegetables. Most men would give their soul for a potato, properly cooked. To ensnare a man's soul, get him boiling with his jacket on, and as soon as the jacket starts to come off, extract every drop of moisture. When he is dry again, return him to the fire until he is quite done.

You may mash them with turnips, onions, leeks, cabbages, fish and meat; you may fry them whole, sliced or in strips. You may roast them, make scones or omelettes or cheesecakes of them, or have them cold with salad. There is nothing your potato cannot do.

When mashing potatoes, most folk make the mistake of adding cold milk with the butter. This makes the mash stodgy and lumpen and you should always ensure that your milk is hot, and your elbow like lightning with the fork. Good mashed potatoes should be fluffy, not stuffy.

If your potatoes are watery, score their jackets along and across and all the way round, salt the water, and when you boil them the jackets will open and release the moisture, ensuring you avoid that soapy wetness that is the death of any potato.

If they be new and you wish their skins off, soak them in salted water before scraping or peeling, and the jackets will the more easily be removed.

Post coitum omne animal triste: Post-Coital Tristesse

But this much depends upon the coition, the coalition, and the practitioners. The notion that all animals are sad after intercourse is a silly and unprovable generalisation, and although the classical author is unknown, almost certainly a male idea. Coition is an animal activity, indicative of our kinship with the beasts; and no animal has answered that it was depressed following intercourse, if the question was ever put. But the saying originates in an incontrovertible truth: that many (not all) men are *indifferent* (not sad) after intercourse, coition having served its elemental purpose of physical release, whereupon a woman has become nothing more than a receptacle, to be discarded or neglected following use. Men rarely confess to this but concoct some lie, but this is a fact of life, for which you should be prepared, if not accustomed. It is true that you may feel a certain 'tristesse', and this is a natural sensation where your reach has failed to exceed your grasp – or what's a heaven for? But if you do not feel infinite fulfilment rather than sadness, after coition, then change the coitioner!

Prayer

Bended knees and clasped hands and shut eyes do not make a prayer. A good dish, humbly but carefully prepared for your family, is a prayer. A kind word in the street, a gentle thought in the dark, these are prayers more eloquent than anything you may hear from the priest.

Predict Weather at Breakfast, To

Drop a sugar lump into your morning coffee and observe the behaviour of the air bubbles that follow. Bubbles forming in the centre of the cup presage good weather; bubbles ringed around the circumference of the cup presage rain, hail or snow; bubbles floating freely and separately reflect a similar uncertainty in the weather. This may seem as absurd as telling a fortune from tea leaves, but has often been proved an infallible method of prognostication.

Pregnancy Test, A

The old folk said that if you urinated on some barleycorn and caused it to grow, it was confirmation that a babe was growing in your belly, but that the urine of a woman without child would prevent the growth. If you are pregnant, the growth will be seen very quickly. Pregnant or not, you may pee among the vegetables, but not directly so, especially to promote carrots. The rhubarb patch will also benefit and the stalks swell red and large. You may also add your urine to the compost heap, and this may be done directly and in the manner that is convenient to you.

Quince

Make the juice of the ripe fruit into a syrup with sugar, which is excellent for the stomach, to stop the vomiting. The green fruit is astringent and restrains diarrhoea. You may use the mucilage externally as an emollient application to cracked lips and nipples.

Rabbit, Stewed

Put the rabbit into a pan with some sweet herbs and 6 cloves, some pepper and allspice, 2 large onions and a roll of lemon peel. Cover with water, skim, simmer for two hours or until tender, make some thick gravy, adding flour and butter rubbed and stirred well in. Boil for ten minutes then sieve it over the rabbit.

Radish

Nothing works more speedily by urine, or brings the little stones away more successfully. Crush the roots and put the fresh juice into a little white wine. This will break up the gravel; but to take it you must possess a good digestion.

Rain

Always keep a rain-barrel and wash your hair in rainwater. Listen to it too, for it induces reflectiveness, though the poets have not written well on the subject, with one modern exception:

Rain, midnight rain, nothing but the wild rain
On this bleak hut, and solitude, and me
Remembering again that I shall die
And neither hear the rain nor give it thanks
For washing me cleaner than I have been
Since I was born ...

Reading

After Homer and the Scriptures, read all of Shakespeare, Milton and the Romantic writers, including especially the late Lord Tennyson. Mrs Browning wrote better verse than her husband. Miss Austen wrote elegant English, and Mrs Gaskell meant well and did moderately, but neither goes to the soul.

Read Dickens and Stevenson but not Thackeray and Trollope, unless you are sure of a long, tedious life. Of foreign authors read Dante, Cervantes, Tolstoy, and all the French you can lay your hands on. These are the greatest.

Of women writers, read Miss Dickinson and the Brontë sisters, best of all Emily, the true poet of Haworth. The Brontës show you what you may do in spite of men, because of men, and without men; and Emily goes straight to soul and bone:

> *I know Miss Brontë's agony,*
> *I know Miss Brontë's soul,*
> *I feel her deep and virgin needs*
> *In the cold Haworth soil.*

Reality

Much talked of by philosophers. But what is it? A sharp wind, that ruffles all day long a little bitter pool about a stone, on a bare coast, watched by a bundle of bones, the one truth that underlies all your ailments, arts and aspirations. When people trouble you, remember that reality, and picture them walking, acting and attitudinising as they do, first without their clothes and then without their flesh. For that is the one truth that lies under all others: a skeleton.

Recognition in Eternity

This is an imponderable question, and you do not know what exactly you will see, or how it will be when you meet.

Yet meet we shall, and part, and meet again,
Where dead men meet on lips of living men.

Reincarnation

This is a word which will do as well as any other to describe what happens to your immortal soul after the death of your body. First, there is absolutely nothing in the Bible to suggest that your birth is the beginning, or that your death is the end of you. Instead you are told two things quite plainly. One is that 'that which is to come hath already been, and that which hath been is yet to come'. There is no new thing under the sun. When you lift your wine glass to your lips, reflect for a moment that the glass is older than you are, though you purchased it only yesterday, for it is composed of substances older than you, materials manufactured from the earth, matter that has always been there, drawn quite literally from the sands of time, and it is the same with human beings. You have an age, so-called, which has been allotted to you at your birth, but has nothing to do with your real age. Lord Tennyson puts it memorably when he writes, 'The star that rises at our birth hath had elsewhere its setting'.

The other piece of evidence from the Bible is given by Christ himself, who pointed to John the Baptist and announced that this was none other than Elijah come back. Nothing could be clearer than that. He told them plainly that the one prophet had returned in the person of another, the same soul clothed in different flesh, no new thing.

As for animals, how could you believe that they will not be resurrected also? Why would God create something only to pronounce it worthless and not worth preserving?

It makes no sense. Animals are your brothers and sisters in the creation and you are no more important in or to the creation than the least of them.

Resignation

Put by the months like mothballs
Forgotten in the drawers...

Respect

This is what you owe to the living: to the dead you owe only truth.

Rest

You will rest well enough when you are dead. For now keep active, and keep death waiting.

Rowan

It is not a log tree, but plant one in the garden, or as close to the house as you can, to keep off the dark ones, and the 'instruments of darkness'. Rowan jelly is delicious, and a tree that bears a heavy crop with regularity is certain evidence that one of great virtue lies buried nearby, rather as Omar says of his rose bush.

I sometimes think that never blows so red
The Rose as where some buried Cæsar bled;
That every Hyacinth the Garden wears
Dropt in its Lap from some once lovely Head.

And this delightful Herb whose tender Green
Fledges the River's Lip on which we lean—
Ah, lean upon it lightly! for who knows
From what once lovely Lip it springs unseen!

Rue

With rue my heart is laden,
For golden friends I had,
For many a rose-lipt maiden
And many a lightfoot lad.

Have no regard for its sorrowful name, for in spite of it, it is a herb of happiness. It will calm hysterics and provoke difficult menstruation, curing any nervous disorder which may accompany the time of the month, especially if you suffer cramps and pains, or if you undergo anger or anxiety of the undetermined sort. Rue is the feminine friend, and you may either drink the infusion or inject it when the stimulant is needed. The fresh juice of the leaves will heal dogbites and bad cuts, or you may apply it to the temples to relieve a headache. A decoction in wine should be gargled for scurvy in the gums, and it will also strengthen the womb and cure disorders in the brain.

It is an old wives' tale that it discourages conception. For discomfort (but not piles) in the back passage, pour 1 pint of boiling water over 2 teaspoons of dried rue; let it simmer for five to ten minutes, and when the infusion is sufficiently cool, apply by bathing. If the discomfort is in the rectum, inject with an eyedropper or pipette. It may prove difficult to treat oneself in this area, and a second party may be required, if the patient will be content to leave modesty well behind.

Rum Omelette

Break into a basin 3 whole eggs, 3 tablespoonfuls of cream, 1 oz castor sugar, and beat all together. Cook in the usual way until the omelette starts to set, then dish it. Pour over the caramel and 2 tablespoonfuls of rum, and set alight just before serving.

The caramel: ¼ oz sugar, 2 tablespoonfuls lemon juice. Boil till golden brown, and serve.

Safe Slimming

There is a great craze on these days, especially among the younger women, for slimming their bodies down to a slip and a shadow, and this can prove detrimental to their health. For safe slimming you should observe the following rules: steam your fish, poach your eggs, boil or bake your tatties, and cook your meat anyway you like, but without sauces, crumbs or flour. Take your soup clear, your fruit fresh, and your vegetables without mayonnaise or oil. Preserves and puddings are forbidden fare, and never go near the dairy. As for your wine, drink it dry, but not the cellar.

However, a sensible young woman will not maintain this regime for more than a month without variation or respite, and a woman who studies the Old Masters will not undertake such a regime at all, for if you look at the bellies and backsides of those women who pleased the eyes of those painters who understood the rules that applied to female perfection, it is perfectly obvious that they never suffered a slimming diet in their lives. A man does not dance round a maypole, nor does he wish to take a lamp post to bed.

Salt

The Italian women say that kissing a man without a moustache is like eating soup without salt: the Italian men say that it increases their women's appetites. You must first kiss a man with a moustache to know what it is that you are missing. You have only to eat an egg without salt to know the huge effect of such a small ingredient; only a grain or two will alter the character of a dish and enhance both appetite and enjoyment.

Leaving aside its essentiality in cooking, salt has many other uses. It will: cure sore throats if gargled in water; aid the digestion; relieve heartburn, burns and bee stings; remove stains from clothes and carpets; dissolve ink stains, and ice on pavements; brighten silverware; kill slugs and weeds; blot fresh writing; invigorate the brain.

Omit salt from your porridge at breakfast and you will all day discover the lack. Salt at breakfast sharpens your wits for the remainder of the day's business; without it a man is a dull dog and you are a sluggish bitch. With it you will write quicker. If we could learn the dietary habits of the great writers we should discover that there were none who failed to salt their food. Eat salt and sparkle, and be the salt of the earth.

Scott

You should read Scott instead of Austen. But with the exception of one or two novels such as *Ivanhoe*, which may delight a reader of twelve or thirteen, Scott should not be read by persons under thirty. The Wizard of the North did not always write because he wanted to, but in order to make money and defray a debt, so while there are great novels on a level with the greatest works of literature, there are some extremely poor ones too.

Seven Years Ketchup

To make a ketchup to keep seven years, take 2 quarts of the oldest strong beer you can get that you have kept hidden. Put to it 1 quart of red wine, ¾ of a pound of anchovies, 3 oz of shallots peeled, ½ an oz of mace, the same of nutmegs, ¼ of an oz of cloves, 3 large races of ginger. Cut in slices, boil all together over a moderate fire till ⅓ is wasted, and the next day bottle it for use. If you be suddenly widowed it will last you till you remarry.

Sexual Intercourse

An activity which men pursue more than women, desiring it for itself, whereas a woman values the man the more. Before marriage it is termed fornication but may be a frequent and necessary matter between lovers as it seals the covenant over and over, keeping them together, a strong cement of the heart. During pregnancy you may continue to have intercourse, but as your belly increases, you should do so with less fervour and more restraint, for the sake of the foetus. But children born of parents who have continued to have intercourse during pregnancy will have a greater degree of sensuality than those who have refrained.

After marriage, and especially after children, be neither surprised nor concerned should intercourse lose its frequency. It has become less necessary. Marriage is the Great Seal, and under it you may both unbend and be easy, knowing that you now belong together in that great bond, with shared goals and stresses that bind you all the more. And even if you do remain devoted and in love, intercourse will be a less frequent event because it is no longer the cementing element, these other seals having been set on your mutual life. Intercourse may eventually become a rare occurrence. No longer the driving force as the daily bread of your togetherness, it may fade into a gentle and occasional reminder that you continue to exist for one another.

Did Adam and Eve have sex before the Fall? No. We are told precisely that Adam knew his wife *after* the Fall. This does not mean that sex in itself is sinful, simply because it belongs only to our sinful state and not to the pre-lapsarian. Fallen man, after all, is capable of great things, even noble things, and so is fallen woman. So those who say that we are rotten to the core and that our sexuality is part of that rottenness, are fools.

Very likely sex was not necessary before the Fall because all was perfection. Now however, in our imperfect lives, we need sex: essentially for procreation (which was unnecessary for a couple who were immortals in Eden, death being the punishment for disobedience) and also for pleasure. After all, even our Lord Jesus Christ teaches us to ask for such a humble item as our daily bread. And sex is like bread. What would life be without it? A dull business indeed.

Sighing

Sighing is said to shorten your life, like kissing and intercourse, which involve a surrender of breath, of the soul, and of the stuff of life. This is superstition. As you kiss and copulate, doubtless you will sigh, and all three are good for you.

Singing

A fine voice is not essential, but singing is conducive to health. Learn operatic arias, and deliver them to no other audience than yourself. It is not the performance that matters, but the physical release of spirits, which is a cleanser of your whole being. People who never sing nourish unhealthy spirits in their blood. Choose Italian and French composers such as Bizet, Gounod, Saint-Saëns, Verdi, Puccini, and Giordano. Wagner is great but difficult; Mozart is great but over-elegant. You must sing with your soul: *Un bel di vedremo, La mamma morta, Mon coeur s'ouvre à ta voix* (that last is the greatest of all songs); and sing them in their language. To sing a French or Italian aria in English is like trying to swim in the sand, while the whole ocean lies before you.

Sleep

The quality and degree of sleep varies hugely according to the age, ability, constitution, and habit of the sleeper. Stupid people need more sleep than those whose minds and intellects are constantly stimulated to such a degree that sleep is an irritating constriction and a regrettable cessation of their endeavours. Consequently it is impossible to specify a suitable period of sleep for all parties.

Too much sleep blunts the mind and body and disposes them to torpor. You will become flabby, listless, and dull. It is entirely possible that those who sleep away their time may live longer lives than those who spend their hours active and alert, but their lives are less worth living, as true experience is a matter of intensity not duration.

As for the quality, an unsound sleep arises from a variety of causes: e.g. disordered bowels; too full a stomach; too much alcohol; anxiety; intense mental activity; heat, cold, light, noise; in the case of ladies, unsatisfied sexual desire, which men may better deal with in the way that is given to them; and in some persons by the use of coffee or green tea. The best narcotic medicines, if they be required to bring on sleep, and the most generally useful, are opium and in their various preparations, henbane and hemlock.

Smoking

Smoking is good for the health. Recent experiments have shown that smoke from strong tobacco kills microbes in the teeth, and after a good smoke the mouth remains sterilised for some hours. In particular the cholera and diphtheria microbes succumb readily to tobacco smoke and in general smoking acts as a deterrent against illnesses. This has now been concluded by the Institute of Bacteriology; and as your microbes are doubtless the same as any man's, you are as entitled to smoke as he is, and as entitled to preserve your own health in this excellent fashion.

But if you are to smoke, you should ensure that the tobacco you use is of a good strong quality. The use of weak tobacco may simply warm up the microbes and encourage them to multiply, producing the effect opposite to the one intended and desired. Stay healthy with a good strong smoke.

Softening of the Member

This can occur well before a man's old age, even in his youth and prime, for it can be brought on by anxiety, fatigue, nerves and drink, even by sexual excitement itself, which may be too much to endure or sustain. You need have no fears that his body has grown weary of yours, most men being desirous of intercourse at almost any time. It is not the desire but the performance which may be lacking, and if you have the deep need in you, or wish to put him at ease, do as nature tells you, and you will find the way to make him capable of you.

Sore Breasts

Bathe your breasts with fleawort or pepper vinegar. If this fails, apply a poultice of lily root made thick with ginger, or slippery elm bark. This should bring the swelling to a head without any pain. Or, you may fry parsley leaves in butter and apply them to your breasts if they be hard, which will mollify them.

Sore Nipples

Make a tea of raspberry leaves and bathe your nipples tenderly. You may add sugar and milk and drink the infusion also. Or, you may apply the juice of the root of comfrey, laid on direct, or boiled in wine. They are more effectual than the leaves. Or, you may use Herb Robert or Stinking Cranesbill, applying an ointment made of the green leaves and lard.

Sore Throat

Mash up raw onions with lemon juice and sugar, or boil them in molasses. Or, boil oak bark for some minutes, strain, allow to cool, then gargle. Or, mix lemon juice from a warmed lemon with honey and glycerine, shake and bottle, and take by the teaspoon. Or, mix honey and sulphur and vinegar, then gargle. Or, make a big pot of red pepper tea with 2 teaspoons of salt, and sweetened up with honey. Strain and gargle while still warm.

If your sore throat results in a lost voice, add the lemon juice of one fruit to the white of 1 egg, and beat up with some castor sugar thrown in to make it palatable. Take frequently by the teaspoon.

Or, you need 1 oz of marshmallow root and 1 oz of honey mixed in a pint of water. Use as a gargle as often as you like. Saltwater is another good gargle, if not so pleasant. Lemon juice in warm water is more palatable if not so effective. Follow one with the other if you like.

Or, simply rub turpentine or goose fat over your chest and throat. Or, heat up a good quantity of salt, put it into a rag or a woollen stocking which has been heated by the fire, and wrap this around the neck. The one burning will oust the other.

Soul, The

The immortal part of yourself that never dies and was never born, but passed into you at your conception. 'Whence camest thou and whither goest thou?' Not knowing the answers to these two questions is what makes birth and death such large adventures. The soul is what is missing when you kiss the corpse, the flicker and flame of life. It is neither consciousness, character, singularity, spirit, mind nor wit. The soul is indefinable. It has passed beyond the moon. Its flight is infinite, it is the irretrievable ingredient that makes you a dish fit for the gods. Without it you are worms' meat. The soul is the summer butterfly that cannot be caught but flies away; its little wings never winter, and are dusted with immortality.

Yet there are some who, in all other respects alive, exhibit a complete lack of soul. They will never sing like the poets, paint like the Masters, or smile like a child. They will never say an interesting word, or even lift an arm like a wave of the sea. They have a shark's aspect; their deadness lies in the eye, the index to the soul. Waste not one second with such like: your time here is precious and your soul priceless. It is what people will remember you by. You cannot cross a room or even lift a finger without revealing your immortality; and when folk imagine that they are recalling you for the glory of your hair or the dimple in your smile, it is your soul that is expressing itself, and it is your soul that they remember, not the rubbish that you leave behind, under some mouldering stone.

Sperm

A man's sperm is good for a woman's skin, anywhere on the body; rubbed in to back and belly it is good for the kidneys and bowels and keeps them warmly clad, especially through the winter, when all pipes must be lagged. On the face too, from time to time, it makes for a clear complexion, though here you should wait a few seconds, gather, and apply, rather than receive it stinging hot, straight from the penis.

Some women boke and cannot bring themselves to swallow it; but swallowed, if you can control yourself, it gives you strength. Nowhere in the bible forbids the consumption of sperm. Onan's trespass (Genesis 38) does not tell us that it is a perversion for a man to spill his sperm outside his wife. Onan was ordered by God to raise up seed to his dead brother by going in unto his widow. This was Jewish law. He was struck dead by God because he neglected his legal duty to produce children for his brother. God was not concerned with where he put his sperm, merely that it was not in the place necessary by that particular law. So you are free to swallow your husband's sperm for your strength's sake.

And as for taking a man's member into your mouth, this may sometimes prove a necessary step if he falters, so that the seed may eventually be sown in the appointed place. If pleasure is essential to erection then this is not ungodly. However, the constant swallowing or spillage of sperm, though not wicked, is surely a sterile and stubborn pursuit.

173

Spirits, Lowness of

The leaves of the beech will lift your spirits, and lavender flowers and germander and wormwood, a bitter tonic with a sweet reward; and also the bitter aloes, especially excellent for lowness, as they stimulate action on the rectum and the uterus.

Stars

O stars, pure stars! Why cannot we emulate your almost timeless calm, the vast mass of your serene beauty, but instead fill a ridiculously small world with such a disproportionate amount of evil: hatred, envy, anger, greed, deceit, wars, murders, molestations and rapes? Why not your peace and dignity and mystery and majesty? Why do we pollute this huge and blameless universe with our ugliness? Such is human nature. The heart is deceitful above all things, desperately wicked. Only the stars are pure.

O stars, pure stars! You gaze alike upon the just and the unjust, but only the innocent of heart and the chaste of soul can understand you, can love you; and you know them too, those who know how to love, for only you are pure, and you alone know how to console.

Stoicism

Read the Emperor Marcus Aurelius. Although the infamous Earl Russell has called him a pitiable figure, this was the noblest Roman of them all, and you should study his *Meditations*. They will teach you when trouble comes not to say that this is misfortune, but that to bear it well is *good* fortune. Things are as they are. Why should you wish them otherwise? And if you can tolerate yourself, then surely you can put up with anything.

Tea

This is a peasant in the princely presence of the great coffee beverage, and not equal to cocoa or chocolate. It exerts an injurious influence on the stomach, bowels and nerves, according to Dr Graham, an opinion to be shared and agreed, and is drunk in this country much too often and much too strong. The green tea especially affects some people in nearly the same degree as digitalis. Whereas the civilisation of France resides in strong coffee and good wine, tea is the English poison. If you must drink it, do so in small quantities.

Tears

Jesus wept. Tears are not the prerogative of women but of all humanity. As laughter and singing are good for the constitution, so indeed are tears, without which injurious emotions would be pent up, mining unseen, causing ulcers and other illnesses and infections of the mind. Better to cry than to go mad.

Teething

Give the bairn dill water or chamomile. You can always add a dash of magnesia.

Time

You do not have it; you never have it; for it flows like water, and the passing moment is nobody's. Time is an illusion. The Egyptians say that time laughs at everything but the pyramids laugh at time. But time antiquates antiquities and even the pyramids will have their day. If you wish to spend your time wisely you should embrace natural time and not man-made, as the poet Marvell advises:

How well the skilful gardener drew
Of flowers and herbs this dial new!
Where, from above, the milder sun
Does through a fragrant Zodiac run;
And, as it works, th' industrious bee
Computes its thyme as well as we.
How could such sweet and wholesome hours
Be reckon'd but with herbs and flowers!

Toads

They are the living jewels of your garden, for they live on the very vermin that threaten to destroy your produce, and you should ensure that you keep special places for them alone: dark, damp and seclusive places, to which they may repair from the garish eye of day, especially if the sun be hot. Moreover they are gentle beings, who have neither the desire nor the means to hurt you, and if you find one on a country excursion you should befriend him and bring him home with you with great care, for a slight injury to another animal does great harm to a toad. Be gentle to him, and he will be the great guardian of your cucumbers in their frames, where he will sit like a dragon devouring all slugs. With such a friend you will never see another pest.

Tobacco, British Herb

If you wish it, the principal ingredients are: dried coltsfoot leaves, to which you must add a smaller portion of thyme, wood betony, eyebright, rosemary and yarrow.

Truth

'What is truth?' said jesting Pilate, and would not stay for an answer. But you do not know that Pilate was jesting, when he may well have been cynical or sad, or in search of truth himself, but in all respects serious. He asked the question of Jesus, whereupon he turned on his heel and walked away. It is not an action that denotes a jest. Perhaps he was an actor, as are we all, but knew it, as many do not.

'To thine own self be true' is the best advice on truth. Then you may live with your Lesbia, and though the sager sort your deeds reprove, you weigh them not – and live with whom you choose.

Unhappiness

Unhappiness is caused by loss: either the loss of what you had and no longer have, or of what you never had and therefore feel the loss of, or the lack of. To avoid it, you

Urine

must not wish for anything, which is impossible, as man cannot live by bread alone. Therefore to be human is to be unhappy. Accept it as your condition – and be content.

Urine

'Not that which goeth into the man, but that which cometh out of the man, that defileth the man,' said Jesus, though he was speaking of bad thoughts and deeds, whereas the food and drink that go in are expelled through the draught, and there is nothing unclean about pee. It possesses certain medical properties and powers. It may be used in an emergency to take the pain out of stings and may be of help in the cure of conditions such as jaundice. It may be gargled to clear throat infections or drunk to cure gout. It may be used as a hair-wash to give a healthy tingle to the scalp and a good gloss to the locks. It may be applied to piles, or used as a fertiliser to swell vegetables, carrots especially, which will be enlarged by your efforts. Lawns are greenest that are constantly sprinkled with urine, though even in the case of a small lawn the whole household must be required to participate.

It may also be used to keep bad spirits out of the house, if applied to the front and back doors, or the doorposts. The best method of application is simply to pee on these direct, as the pee is more potent when hot and fresh. Stale pee has no effect. This is easier work for a man, unless you can spout like a whale.

Valerian

Dried and drunk, it will bring on your periods, clear your eyes, calm your nerves, allay anxieties, dispel stones, cure headaches, banish insomnia, and help you pee.

Vaseline

No lady should be without a tub of Vaseline. It is a matchless emollient and complexion preserver and may prove useful in a variety of situations, troublesome or pleasurable.

Venereal Diseases

If you wish to be certain of avoiding this condition you must use the absolute preventative method, which is total abstinence from intercourse with men – or women. This being against nature, a less extreme circumspection would consist in your choice of company. In this regard, though you can scarcely avoid seaports if you wish to travel, you need not consort with seafaring men who, after long absences from shore, indulge themselves freely but not cleanly, especially with women whose trade thrives in these very ports and among these same men. But be under no misapprehension: the saintliest 'he' alive may furnish you with a venereal disease, even if he be your husband, and a marriage bond is no preventer of the pox. Never embark on relations with any man until or unless you have first examined him privately; and by this token you must insist on light in the first instance, after which, if you are satisfied all is in order, you may proceed without it.

Vinegar and Brown Paper

For a cold in the chest, for a sore throat, a sore back, or any bruise or soreness, steep *thick* brown paper in the vinegar and apply to the afflicted area. If you have a coat that is too thin to keep out the winter cold you may lay thick brown paper between the lining and the outer material and stitch it in, where it will add extra warmth without extra weight. This should also be done in winter to quilts that have worn thin, and they may be lined with it, or it may be used as backing to protect families from the most bitter weather.

Violet

Young violets are antiseptic and are excellent for inflammations of the arse: make a decoction of the leaves and flowers with water and wine, and with this cooling liquor bathe the fundamental parts. The flowers are a gentle laxative, and a good poultice for the piles can be made out of the green leaves. The syrup of violets relieves chest coughs and tightness. To make it, take a quantity of the flowers, pour boiling water over them sufficient to cover them, and let it stand all night. In the morning strain, and add sugar, two pounds to each pint, and melt over the fire. This is a good gentle purge for young children.

WEEPERS AND SWEEPERS

Wars are made by busy men
Just an hour or more,
Women do the clearing up –
Loss a longer chore.

When your boy has done his bit
And lies on foreign plain,
Sit out your life on window seats –
Watch the falling rain.

If the broken bits they brought
Lie under yonder leaf,
Fit with your heart, cross-stitch the grass,
Take time to mend your grief.

Leaders have no time for us,
Heroes do as must –
We are the sweepers-up
Of centuries of dust.

[One of Elspeth's compositions, others appearing on pages 138, 156, 159 and 187.]

Warning to Sirens

Try to be true, for though men were deceivers ever, sirens too will have their day.

> *Prime youth lasts not, age will follow*
> *And make white these tresses yellow;*
> *Wrinkled face for looks delightful*
> *Shall acquaint the dame despiteful;*
> *And when time shall date thy glory*
> *Then too late thou wilt be sorry.*
> *Siren pleasant, foe to reason,*
> *Cupid plague thee for thy treason.*

Water Fern

The decoction of the root in white wine gives the uterus a good scouring and makes you pee.

Wealth

Do not long for it: it is harder to leave behind you than want, as obscurity is easier to relinquish than fame.

Aspire instead to be rich in knowledge, to be wealthy in wit, and in kindness, courtesy, compassion and understanding. True riches lie in self-reliance, and in loving those who rely on *you*.

Wedding Night

If you are wise you will not have allowed him to see you naked before now, no matter what intimacies you may have known together. This is important, for it is always a great and pleasurable shock to a man to see the woman he has known for years stand unclothed before him now. There is simply so much more of you than he has imagined. But when the moment comes, do it not slowly but suddenly, so that the shock is all the greater. He must remember this ever afterwards.

And afterwards, if you are a virgin, keep the bloodstained sheets you slept in as a testimony to your intactness and truth. Being a man, yours will not have been the first field he has ploughed, and if in time he grows jealous and accuses you, thrust the sheets in his face and let your immaculate blood speak for you better than any lawyer. Abel's blood spoke against Cain from the ground, and yours will speak from the wedding sheets.

Welsh Rarebit

You need:

> *bread, 2 slices*
> *cheese, ¼ lb cheddar*
> *milk, 2 tablespoonfuls*
> *mustard, ½ teaspoonful*
> *1 egg*

Grate your cheese, place it in a small pan, add the eggs, milk and mustard, and bring to the boil. When ready, pour onto the bread, toasted and buttered, and serve cut into nice wee squares.

White Hairs

Old age will snow white hairs on you, but if you do not wish this to happen before the evil days, put a pinch of iron sulphate from the chemist into a good big glass of red wine. Mix, pour into a wide soup bowl, and dip your comb into it over and over while you comb your hair for a good quarter of an hour. Do this twice a week and you may never sit under a head of white hairs.

And yet, consider how gruesome you will look, with your raven locks framing an old wrinkled monkey's skin, unless you have taken the cure for wrinkles too. And for keeping tired eyes bright, and so on. But then your turkey's neck will give you away, as will your crabby hands, your corky arms and your prune-stone elbows. And even if you have spent countless time and energies seeing to the mending and prevention of all this, what about your wrinkled insides, your slipped and shrunken organs and your weary soul? A wise woman goes with nature and prepares for death with dignity, and with sense appropriate to her age.

Wild Marjoram

Sometimes it was sown on graves to give joy to the dead. To the living it is a strong healer, being a powerful antidote to hemlock, henbane and opium. It removes acidity from the stomach, relieves toothache and headache, deafness, dropsy and scurvy, and promotes the menstrual flow.

Wind

A blue wind's roaring through the woods,
It doesn't stop to say,
O where it's bound or whence it came,
Or who will die today.

My own. Listen to the wind, especially as you walk or sit alone, and especially in the darkness with no lamp on or gas lit. You will learn much from the sounds of the wind concerning the quest of life and the apparent aimlessness of existence as it will appear to you at times, for as the Bible says, 'the wind bloweth where it listeth and thou hearest the sound thereof, but canst not tell whence it cometh nor whither it goeth'; and in that respect the wind is a perfect image of the human life. Where did you come from? And where are you going to? These are the only two questions worth considering, for in between these two great imponderables is a brief affair; and by listening to the wind your little vessel will be pushed out on the sea of contemplation, even as you sit in your chair. If you return from that voyage not with answers but even with questions in your head and sensations in your soul, you have been befriended by the wind. The best poem on the wind was written by Shelley. Read his *Ode to the West Wind*. O wind! If winter comes, can spring be far behind?

Wind, Medical

For wind in the stomach, take a large handful of feverfew and cumin seeds and ginger, one ounce of each, to three quarts of water; boil down to half the quantity, that is three pints. The dose is three or four wine glassfuls a day.

Or take oil of juniper, tincture of myrrh, lavender water, sweet nitre, an equal quantity of each: shake them in a bottle. Dose: a teaspoonful in a cup of cold water, this being the dose for an adult.

Woman

Defined in the old days as beasts of burden, chattels at best, and at worst receptacles for filth, women are in truth the cradle of civilisation. We push out from our bellies emperors and idiots, sometimes one and the same, we suckle them, rear them, bind hard families together, feed and nurse, clean and care, fall on our backs, open our legs wide for men and midwives, then we dress our dead and die ourselves, often unregarded. And for what? God said that it was not good for a man to be alone, and so he made woman to help him along. But pay no heed to that old helpmate theory, the ethic of a desert tribe. It has suited men in power well enough for centuries to tar us with that brush. Do not believe a word of it. Walk through the world with your nostrils to the stars, your nipples thrust before you, and your head held high. Men are the glory, jest and riddle, but you are the one living wonder of the world, and the other seven are just history.

THE W.H.K & S. ELLEN TERRY CORSET.

Work

It may be Adam's curse but it is Eve's also and you are part of it. Why complain? An animal must hunt. If you do not work, you have no right to eat.

Worms, To Cure With Gunpowder

A Child's thimbleful of Gunpowder Bruised in a mortar, & put it to Steep over night in a Large Spoonful of red wine; pour off the clear in the morning & give it to ye Child; give it every other day for nine days.

Wrinkles

Get some lily bulbs and crush them for the juice. Mix 4 oz of this with 4 oz of honey, 2 oz of melted white wax in 2 tablespoonfuls of rosewater. Put on this mask last thing at night and remove in the morning. Or, simply apply olive oil each evening before bed especially before intercourse. The Greek men used to oil their bodies in this way all over before intercourse, believing it enhanced the pleasure. Doubtless it did – but they never had to wash the sheets in the morning.

Youth

Never does youth understand its own insignificance, or know how to wait.

Youth, To Preserve

Let all your meats be dressed rare and not too much done, for if their juices be out of them, the stomach is not pleased with them. Experience daily testifies that Jews and Frenchmen and women who eat all their food over dressed, look even whilst young so yellow, dry, wrinkled, and as it were withered (so that an old Englishman or woman looks better than they), and in age look extremely hagged, beyond all manner of expression.

Acknowledgements

I want to thank Michael O'Mara for his immediate interest in what he saw of Epp's writings; and his enthusiasm has been amply continued by my marvellous editor, Louise Dixon who got to the heart of Epp right from the start and has steered the course of this book with absolute sympathy and understanding.

I should also like to thank Miss Jane Errington and Miss Meme Errington of Earlsferry, for showing me their own Family Receipt Book, which played a large part in my decision to publish Epp's Guide.

Like Epp, though for different reasons, I am computer illiterate, and I owe a huge debt to Miss Rachel Brown and to my wife Anna, for the long hours they spent helping me to decipher and transcribe Epp's manuscripts. The subsequent hours of typing were also all theirs. And thanks also to West Port Print St Andrews, whose fast and friendly facilities have helped me see this book and many another through the press.

More of Epp's writings await the light of day, but all might have been lost to posterity but for the quiet preservations of my late dear mother – and that little brown suitcase which contained so much! And finally there is Epp herself, born in the nineteenth century, and whose penwork has allowed readers of the twenty-first to enter into her obscure existence and share her many responses to the wonders of life.

C.R.